Urban Poetry from China

Urban Poetry from China

Selected by Huang Fan & James Sherry

Translations edited by Daniel Tay

ROOF BOOKS
NEW YORK

ISBN: 978-1-931824-93-4
Library of Congress Control Number: 2021930646

This project is supported, in part, by an award from the National Endowment for the Arts.

This book is made possible by the New York State Council on the Arts with the support of the Office of the Governor and the New York State Legislature.

Roof Books
are published by
Segue Foundation
300 Bowery, New York, NY 10012
seguefoundation.com

Roof Books
are distributed by
Small Press Distribution
1341 Seventh Street
Berkeley, CA. 94710-1403
800-869-7553 or spdbooks.org

Table of Contents

Preface: Are China's Cities the "New Great Wall"?

Huang Fan

Translated by Benjamin Orion Landauer

Urban poetry in China has served as a unique witness of this new millennium, reaching a depth and charm that other forms of writing have yet to attain. On one hand, the urban forest draws us into a haven of materialism, inadvertently causing us to stumble into the abysses of human nature. On the other hand, cities attempt to overcome the limits of individuals, a collective effort. And urban poets aspires to leave behind something for the future to read and interpret, since, of course, the object of materialism is not the actual reason we lose sleep at night.

Over her several thousand years of growth, China is no stranger to urbanization. The sudden explosion of pastoral poetry in the Classical Chinese tradition, upon close examination, reveals a thinly veiled sentiment, that is, poets tend to reject the fervor often accompanying urbanization. Instead, they strive to take the stress and clamor imposed on the subject by city life and transform it into reverberating songs of the pastoral. Two hundred years ago, when Goethe described his era with the phrases "modernity" and "the past two ragged centuries," he was referring to the urbanization of contemporary Europe, which, incidentally, is a nice foil to the rapid urban development seen in China's history, particularly that of the Southern Song (1127-1279) and the latter part of the Ming Dynasty (1368-1644). But the urban development seen in China over the past forty years has resulted in an aesthetic response distinctly different from that of the past. Of course, there is still a tendency of Chinese poets to take the stress of city life and transform it into pastoral poetry, a phenomenon noticed and followed by many. However, I focus my attention on a different phenomenon: how do cities enter poetry? This is not a question of tactics, for though cities are a creation of humans, they have already exceeded the realm we can readily control, and now have the seemingly magical power to absorb us—could they really be the Gods of the modern day?

At the beginning of the 1980s, cities were the most desirable place for any Chinese person to be. Forty years later, this psychological mainstay has transformed into a wariness mixed with suspicion, anxiety, and even mourning, since, situated in the whirlpool of "modernity," as it is called, cities don't appear to have transformed into the New Great Wall of Resisting Solitude as once hoped. This psychological shift began at the start of the new millennium. Reading urban poetry from this period is one of the greatest ways to get up-close and personal with this shift. Since this type of urban poetry is an aesthetic response to the severe birth pains of Chinese cities' rampant growth, in addition to the fact that readers have only had a little over ten or so years to seriously read these poems, the poets nearly destined to have mastery over this distinctly novel form are those born in the fifties, sixties, and seventies.

Of course, due to the rapidness of China's economic expansion, social and infrastructural development has been starkly out of balance across her vast territory. Thus, in Chinese urban poetry, readers see a wide variety of different aesthetic responses, which are most definitely not limited to one style. For example, the expressivity so closely associated with farming society has not been completely abandoned, but has rather changed into one of the major veins of contemporary urban poetry in China. The Chinese people's poetry tradition has a history of several thousand years. Among the multiplicity of responses to modern urbanization, Chinese poets transfer expressivity, Chinese imagery, language poetry, a blend of Eastern and Western aesthetics, metaphysical and literal musings, urban and rustic themes, ancient and modern themes, all in an effort to widen and deepen the scope of urban poetry itself. It is full of the pleasure of close examination, a depth of knowledge, and due to the highly emotional and imagistic elements that several poets bring into their work, it includes elements of grief, solitude, and the bizarre. The honesty of this selection of poetry lies in that it does not affectedly cater to the one-note "postmodern" wave of poetics, but instead positions urban poetry between the Eastern and Western, between the ancient and modern, into a new millennium where both the minivan and traffic jams are exceedingly popular—is this not at once a perennial yet fresh experience? Perhaps bearing witness in this way both avoids the arrogance of a one-note poetics, and is further suited to expressing the vast complexities of a heterogeneous China.

This volume collects poetry from the Chinese mainland, Macau, and Taiwan. Due to space restrictions, only the most representative poets of the new millennium could be selected for inclusion, but what this volume provides is far from a comprehensive image—as one poet is included, ten thousand are left out.

—Jiangning Sector, Nanjing City, December 2018

Translation Editor's Preface

Daniel Tay

When people talk about translation, they are justifiably interested in the relationship between source and target texts. The words used to describe this relationship can sometimes reveal how confused people are about it. A translation must be "loyal" and "faithful," yet it must also endeavor to "capture" the original. Translators, then, face the difficult task of writing a text that is both a subset of another text and a superset for it. It seems a translation must be smaller than the original so as to contain nothing that the original does not, yet simultaneously larger than the original so as to include and even comment on it while functioning in a new language.

In this volume, readers will find many excellent translations that attempt to meet this challenging task—ambitious, technically sound, engaging works that at once function with, transmit, deepen, and transgress the meanings of their source texts. Readers will also find equally rewarding translations that attempt to subvert this task entirely. These latter translations embed themselves in an intertextual network, serving as stabilizing nodes that relate as much to their Chinese source texts as they do to other translations and texts in English.

Take, for example, Sun Dong's self-translated "Libertine, Night Guard and Roamer," in which she uses the phrase "The sun also rises." The Chinese original seems to subtly allude to the Hemingway title as well. Since Sun Dong is a fluent English speaker, questions arise: what is the source of the reference? Is it the English version of the Hemingway text, or rather its Chinese translation? And if it is the English version, then could there be an argument that Sun Dong's English poem, with its direct reference to the title, is actually more "original" than her Chinese version?

Or take any one of the Chinese poems in this collection that directly reference older Chinese texts, including Hu Mingming's "Poem Written on Hainan Airlines Menu" (translated by yours truly). This piece refers to the Tang Dynasty poem "Over the Border" by Wang Changling. A different question arises: should the translator quote a previously published English translation, or directly render the quoted text into English? Certainly, this decision is a complex one. Rather than arriving at a one-size-fits-all determination, perhaps the very question suggests that the origins of a translated text are multiple, not as clear as a simply-the-original-in-a-different-language notion would have one believe.

Even when older texts are not directly referenced, similar questions can emerge. Should a translator prioritize the literal meanings of words in a source text, or should their translation prioritize the text's deeper meaning, effect, sound, or poetics? Rendering Chen Dongdong's "Record of an Image" into English, Eleanor Goodman remarkably reimagines his Chinese wordplay. Chen creates a pun on the words for porn (pronounced máopiàn) and Maoist thought (máo sīxiǎng) in a phrase that might be literally rendered "Other people / watched porn, betraying Maoist thought." Gracefully, Goodman translates the phrase "Others / watched soft core porn to oppose the hard left," reconfiguring the play of mao/mao with soft/hard. Her clever maneuver is an act of poetic fidelity, not betraying the original so much as extending and individuating from it.

In a similar way, this collection of Chinese urban poetry extends and distills the love and nature poetry of Chinese tradition into today's tropes. Shen Qi calls for a return to traditional Chinese roots through extensive literary reference in his 29-part excerpted poem "Thereafter," translated by Benjamin Landauer. Part Two of his poem references the Tang poet Du Fu's description of Li Bai by saying, "how haggard is he!" But by Part Ten of the poem, traces of less romantic contemporary city life creep in. Shen Qi discusses anxiety and mortgage payments. Notably, Shen Qi puts the word "mortgage" in quotation marks, as if to suggest its novelty in Chinese society given the advent of residential mortgage lending following the economic reforms of the late 1970s and 1980s. Then, as Landauer translates, "behind every eyeball / *septwolves* roam." *Septwolves* is a popular Chinese clothing and cigarette brand.

Meanwhile, Yen Ai-lin summons nature in her poem "Winter Beyond Clouds, Within Rain," translated by Jonathan Chiang. In a new twist on the Chinese theme of nature described as a kind of self-portraiture, she asks, "Why do today's clouds cry / before wandering?" She then goes on to claim that "a city of poets are downing Prozac." The cases of Shen Qi and Yen Ai-lin clarify that the work of a skilled translator is not only to get Chinese poems into English, but to take stock of how ancient poetry is embedded in the new along the way. Even the recent Misty Poetry of the 20th century ends up embedded within a textual vending machine in Chen Li's imaginative "A Vending Machine for Nostalgic Nihilists," translated by Chang Fen-ling.

In short, rather than considering the English translations in this anthology solely through their relationships to the Chinese originals, I encourage readers to look at these translations as texts in their own right. As Huang Fan shared in an email to me, "Every translator's primary responsibility is to make good poetry." In this light, where there are divergences between source texts and their translations, the editors have worked with translators to make the best possible English version. These translated poems' creative sources are as various, diverse, and far-reaching as those of any other poem and—like the wonderful work brought together in this book—perhaps visible in the many features of the 21st-century Chinese city.

—New York, New York, December 2020

An Qi (安琪)

In the Depth of the Night

In the depth of the night, breathing heavily, you and I
In the depth of the night
Pacing, the way one practices Taiji, left leg, stepping out, pausing, right leg
Stepping out, pausing, keeping a balance
Breathing evenly
The broad back shadow of you, black, like a moving fire, suppressed
In the depth of the night

The weak lamplight shines on things that don't change
The couch hugs the mess of a white quilt
Your clothes in disorder, abandoned on the low back of the chair
One has to persist
I, savagely, stare at you I love you
And you don't believe it

In the depth of the night, the gas switched on, and on again
One must find a decent excuse for death and I don't believe
Death could resolve grace
The oily kitchen
Facing off with the smelly toilet
This is how life persists
In the depth of the night
Persistence is cruelty I want to give up on I want to say to you I love you
And you don't believe it

Toothache hidden in the tooth
The clock was ticking away
The sky dimly lit, the spring still cold
Dear my dear
When I know you spring has arrived
And your silence, consistent like the cold
Persists

Translated by Ouyang Yu

在夜的深处

在夜的深处，呼吸沉重，我和你
在夜的深处
踱步，以太极的方式，左腿，迈，顿，右腿
迈，顿，身体要平衡
气息要均匀
你厚厚的背影，黑色，像一座移动的烈火被按捺在
夜的深处

微弱的光照着不变的一切
长沙发胡乱抱着白被子
你的衣服零乱，丢置在不高的椅背上
不能不坚持
我狠狠的凝视着你我爱你
而你不相信

在夜的深处，煤气开了又关
必须为死亡找到良好的借口而我不相信
死亡能够化解恩怨
油腻的厨房
对峙于味道浓厚的厕所
这就是生的执着
在夜的深处
执着是一种残忍我想放弃想对你说我爱你
而你不相信

牙疼隐含在牙里
时钟滴答
天光微亮，春天寒冷尚未消散
亲爱的亲爱的
当我认识你 春天到了
而你一以惯之的沉默像寒冷
尚未消散

An Qi (安琪)

They Were Talking about Love

They were talking about love, which was a bit absurd.
Do you really think the two
Pieces of silicon you were touching were breasts
And the two slices of lipstick you were kissing were lips
And what you entered was a body
And when you withdrew it was gratification

They were talking, and the lamp was getting cold
And the strange walls were plotting a collapse, the ground plotting a cave-in
A greater calamity was being planned in the air because
    they were talking about love
The plane laughed, crashing, out of control

Translated by Ouyang Yu

他们在说爱情

他们在说爱情，这有点荒唐，难道你以为你摸到的
两个硅胶就是乳房
你吻到的两爿口红就是嘴唇
你进入的就是身体
你出来的就是满足

他们在说，而那盏灯在冷
而陌生的墙壁预谋倒塌，而地预谋陷裂
空中预谋更大的灾难因为他们在说爱情
飞机笑了，控制不住掉了下来。

An Qi (安琪)

Leaves in Beijing

leaves in Beijing,
clean and clean through and through
a tiny, tiny blade
unentangled
leaves in Beijing
all fallen in winter
the spring green, like jade, chilling
the autumn, flash after flash, shaking you
summer
I've forgotten how the leaves looked in summer
summer's Beijing
I didn't take note of them
I was busy
living a life without love

Translated by Ouyang Yu

树叶在北京

树叶在北京干干净净的
一小片一小片
不纠缠
树叶在北京
冬天全部掉落
春天青翠逼人
秋天一闪一闪的晃着你
夏天
夏天的树叶什么样子我忘了
夏天的北京
我没有注意到树叶
我忙碌于
没有情感的生活

An Qi (安琪)

Beginning with July

Already July, when you were texting, you were missing me
In a July that began again, you were in the nearby village texting
Missing me, the cool bamboo mat printed with you and your shadow
Over the close desk the fluorescent light ready to explode
You were texting, missing me, like the landlord, missing her rent

Translated by Ouyang Yu

七月开始

七月了，你在灯下发短信，你在想我
在重新开始的七月你在很近的村庄发短信
想我，身旁的竹凉席印着你和你的影子
很近的桌上日光灯就要炸裂
你在发短信，想我，像房东在想她的房租

An Qi (安琪)

West of Caihuying Bridge

At this point we say: let's turn here, take the feeder road, take a nice long walk
Oh, the road we tread stretches far; the search is arduous; the emotions bitter; the love tiring; the persons and objects
Are hardly worth a cent; our life is past midway; the revolution has already succeeded, or it hasn't yet succeeded, and our trials
Are enough to fill a granary, so bizarre and blessed and inane that we say, What more do you want?
You, you on the road, you who are chasing time, you who are ripe for a whipping and a pummeling by death
You feminist, what more do you want?

We have reached Caihuying; these bridge lanes branching right and left are grafted onto the sky, making level ground
suddenly rear up several meters into the air; now that you've taken to strolling at this point we say: Give yourself a rest
Those tottering buildings changed their features overnight; one night enwreathed in a lone cloud
We saw the moon looking like a leukemia patient, its pallid face chilled and mournful, and one night
A cool wind parted a clump of grass to show our stream of consciousness, a draft in grass characters of a fantasy on a reclining chair
Those passing perplexities, having nagged us enough, now take a fixed shape and are reborn, revealing traces in shifting light and shade

As for we who are still on the road, we pursued by time, who warmly love being alive...
We whose existence is open to doubt, what more could we want?

Translated by Denis Mair

菜户营桥西

自此我们说，可以拐弯了，可以走辅路走路漫漫的路
其路也修远其求索也艰辛其情也苦其爱也累其人其物
不值一文其生已过半其革命已成功或尚未成功其遭遇
也丰硕也奇异也幸福也荒诞那么我们说，你还要什么
你，在路上的你，追赶时间的你，欠死亡抽你揍你的
你，女性主义的你，你还想要什么？

菜户营已到，这左一道右一道的桥嫁接在空中使平地
陡然拔高几米，你转悠其间自此我们说，可以安歇了
那些临近崩溃的楼层在夜晚换了面目，孤云缠绕某夜
我们看见月亮像白血病患者惨淡的脸凄清而哀怨某夜
凉风曝光了草丛中草拟的意识流我们在长椅上的幻想
那些过往的困惑因絮叨而成型而复活落迹于刹那光影

我们，在路上的我们，被时间追赶的我们，热爱活着
的我们，并不存在的我们，我们还能要什么？

An Qi (安琪)

Fathermother Land

See that person headed homeward, his face wreathed in holiday smiles, saying his native place was once the State of Lu
See that person headed homeward, pleased with her success, saying her native place was once the State of Qin

See that crowd of people, lugging a New Year's glow from the capital, hurrying on the homeward road
Saying their hometowns were once in the ancient states of Shu, Wei or Wu

Boundless stretch of mountains and rivers, fought over by succeeding dynasties...so many dukedoms rose and fell, and you ask me
What ancient domain am I from? I say, My native place wasn't found in the Spring and Autumn Period; it wasn't in the Tang Dynasty. It has only one title

Which is "Fathermother Land." My father served as a soldier, worked in a factory, went into business
My father wrote compositions for me, published my poetry collection, stoked my fire and felt my sadness

He said, Go and make your way! O Father, I've dreamed of making my way in the demimonde, then finally staying put

At your side. My mother was a young beauty, born in the wrong era, who won outstanding marks, only to find herself
In the era of the "Great" Cultural Revolution, so she had to settle for a hasty marriage and a hasty pregnancy
Which was me. She said, That's the way life is; it's not about dreams or honor

It's not about your feelings of joy or sorrow. To have stability in this lifetime is happiness. My father and mother
Now dwell in their domain, feeling concern for me, like anyone separated from a loved one in times of turmoil.

Facing towards the South, with deliberate penstrokes I write: Fathermother Land.

Translated by Denis Mair

父母国

看一个人回故乡，喜气洋洋，他说他的故乡在鲁国
看一个人回故乡，志得意满，他说他的故乡在秦国

看这群人，携带二月京都的春意，奔走在回故乡的路上
他们说他们的故乡在蜀国、魏国和吴国

无限广阔的山河，朝代演变，多少兴亡多少国，你问我
我的国？我说，我的故乡不在春秋也不在大唐，它只有

一个称谓叫父母国。我的父亲当过兵，做过工，也经过商
我的父亲为我写过作文，出过诗集，为我鼓过劲伤过心

他说，你闯吧，父亲我曾经也梦想过闯荡江湖最终却厮守
一地。我的母亲年轻貌美生不逢时，以最优异的成绩遇到

“伟大”的革文化命的年代，不得不匆匆结婚，匆匆
生下我。她说，一生就是这样，无所谓梦想光荣

无所谓欢乐悲喜，现世安稳就是幸福。我的父母
如今在他们的国度里挂念我，像一切战乱中失散的亲人

我朝着南方的方向，一笔一划写下：父母国。

Chen Dongdong (陈东东)

August

In August I pass by the piano room of politics, and hear someone practicing a soaring passage over and over

A helicopter drops into shadow
its big dragonfly torso
extends from the eaves of a birdcage

I'm so far gone, I've left the city
I'll leap onto a cement dam a hundred feet high
but the wind at my back
will still carry that soaring passage

The tulips' ears, the ears of an imagined beast
the ears of a herring's shimmering scales
are plugged by the fingers that play the music

In August, I sit atop a dam
and can see the piano room's roof in the distance
the helicopter seems to fly level
with my eyebrows: will it ride
on the soaring passage—
that seems like something a dragonfly would do

Translated by Eleanor Goodman

八月

八月我经过政治琴房，听见有人
反复练习那高昂的一小节

直升飞机投下阴影
它大蜻蜓的上半身
从悬挂着鸟笼的屋檐探出

我已经走远，甚至出了城
我将跃上高一百尺的水泥大坝
我背后的风
仍旧送来高昂的一小节

郁金香双耳，幻想中一只走兽的双耳
鳞光闪闪的鲱鱼的双耳
则已经被弹奏的手指堵塞

八月，我坐到大坝上
能够远眺琴房的屋脊
那直升飞机几乎跟我的双眉
齐平：它是否会骑上
高昂的一小节
——这像是蜻蜓爱干的事

Chen Dongdong (陈东东)

Descent

In its ceremonial descent the swallow's experimentation
is sometimes the spiraling frigatebird's
experimentation as it crosses the seas

While the gasworks' experiments with flying in close
to so-called vertigo is a thundering unexpected
obligatory euphemism

in a fan-shaped field it slows again
along an even more majestic fan-shaped seashore, it
digs in its heels, and two brightly polished

enormous stainless steel containers turn into breasts
that feed the flames, the employment rate
feeds the delta's unconscious infantile ideals

so someone slips from the iron smokestack
like a flag signaling the all-clear
and walks out of the gasworks
and in his identity, the descendants of the last age
join the burning pain and blood of the newborn economy
his mind's eye is still trained

in midair: the swallow and frigatebird
reunite since heavy rain is about to arrive
and the dragonfly, ah, the dragonfly

he slowly walks down the sloping road
and enters the fairly intense
green—the forcefully contracted

village is farther below. There
insomnia serves as grief and hope's
ambiguous euphemism

Translated by Eleanor Goodman

下降

下降仪式里燕子的试探性
有时也会是盘旋中军舰鸟
渡海的试探性

而一座煤气厂试探着飞临了
所谓晕眩，是轰鸣和意外
勉强的委婉语

在扇形田野它再一次减速
在更加壮丽的扇形海畔
它站稳了脚跟，两只锃亮的

不锈钢巨罐将成为乳房
喂养火焰，就业率
喂养三角洲意识空白的襁褓理想

于是有人从铁烟囱滑落
像一面解除警报的旗
他走出煤气厂

身份中混合着末世子孙和
大经济新生儿灼痛的血
他脑中的视域仍在

半空：燕子和军舰鸟
为即将到来的大雨而欢聚的
蜻蜓，啊蜻蜓

他顺着坡道缓缓向下
走进较为浓郁的
绿色——被迫收缩

乡村在更低处。在那里
失眠，是悲哀和期望
含混的委婉语

Chen Dongdong (陈东东)

Window Niche

Now all that's left is a window niche
suspended alone against the presumptive peacock blue horizon
the top of the building opening its mouth to the nothingness
is hard to imagine—it still doesn't reveal
the panthers and tigers of the architect's shocking style

But this can be inferred: through the window niche you
see yourself, riding awkwardly
on a pterodactyl, so are you trying to charge
and vanish into the bright lake of the mirror? Or perhaps
you've merely sat down at the dressing table
with your weary neck drooping like a drowsy cat

So for a second time through the window niche
you can see a mound of brocaded underthings
tossed in disorder, and a lioness reclining in boredom
If the door to some hidden place moves
to reveal an even more hidden backyard, you can

make a prediction, or a supposition: how can you
use the shallow glare on a fish-shaped pond
to guess at the most hidden reflections—a window niche
is like an inverted image, its nothingness
accentuated by the nonexistence of the peacock blue horizon
like imaginary memoirs imagined at that very moment

The test of strength between language and the world is merely
a test of your own strength—the surrealism of the window niche
is already your reality. Dusk
arrives, and takes the afternoon tea away. A colony of bats
returns to the dim illumination of the dressing table mirror. But

you look for confirmation: the silhouette of the architect's
outdoor productions will elongate the stare of the setting sun
and can you see you're looking down at yourself—
not going through it anymore, but slowly stretching out of it—
beyond the window niche is the savagery of words, the night's
wolf pack, merging with daytime reverie

Translated by Eleanor Goodman

窗龛

现在只不过有一个窗龛
孤悬于假设的孔雀蓝天际
张嘴去衔住空无的楼头还难以
想象——还显露不了
建筑师骇人的风格之虎豹

但已经能推测：你透过窗龛
看见自己，笨拙地骑在
翼指龙背上，你企图冲锋般
隐没进映现大湖的玻璃镜？也许
只不过，你刚好坐到梳妆台边上
颈窝里倦曲着猫形睡意

那么又一次透过窗龛
你能够看见一堆锦绣，内衣裤
凌乱，一头母狮无聊地偃仰
如果幽深处门扉正掀动
显露更加幽深的后花园，你就能

预料，你就能虚拟：你怎样
从一座鱼形池塘的肤浅反光里
猜出最为幽深的映像——一个
窗龛如一个倒影，它的乌有
被孔雀蓝天际的不存在衬托
像幻想回忆录，正在被幻想

语言跟世界的较量不过是
跟自己较量——窗龛的超现实
现在也已经是你的现实。黄昏天
到来，移走下午茶。一群蝙蝠
返回梳妆镜晦黯的照耀。而

你，求证：建筑师野外作业的
身影，会拉长凝视的落日眼光
你是否看见你俯瞰着自己
——不再透过，但持久地探出
窗龛以外是词的蛮荒
夜之狼群，混同白日梦

Chen Dongdong (陈东东)

Record of an Image

Offstage. The usher flicks on her flashlight
Samdech Penn Nouth shakes and shakes as he applauds
a news summary: Chairman Mao in his advanced years swims across the Yangtze

A satellite sweeps through the daytime sky above the movie theater
the viewers have their own dark day. Comrade Jiang Qing
accompanies Nixon, studying each other's ballet revolutions

Someone gropes about, exploring under the skirt in the next seat
and the usher flashes her light again. In a clearing
in the woods, Wu Qinghua somersaults over the world

He rides his bicycle like a motorbike, then a motorbike
like a US Army speedboat on the Mekong
goggles reflecting the just-captured steel helmets and camouflage

He used to run films to theaters along imaginary riverbanks, both sides of the street
shifting dimensions. He once recklessly strode back
behind the screen, and the sudden brightness at the end of the show

gradually darkened again, against a tide of wild hair tangled with adornments—
if he'd stopped, he'd be washed away
as the theater filled with some other song from some other movie

*

The film-runner hadn't yet shown up, but two people left
in the middle. They squinted against the bright light
that overflowed with the perplexity of the entire world

They wanted to stop by the cigarette store, then changed their minds
and turned into the People's Park. The grove sifted out
the noontime noise, the branches knitting into a secret sea

影像志

暗场。女领票员拧亮了手电
宾努亲王频频颤抖，颤抖着鼓掌
新闻简报：毛主席高龄横渡了长江

人造卫星掠过电影院上空的白天
观众们各就各自的黑昼。江青同志
陪同尼克松，观摩芭蕾舞剧的革命

有人更去摸索，探向邻座裙底
女领票员又一闪手电。林间
空地上，吴清华跃起世界翻了身

*

他把自行车骑作摩托，又把摩托
开成一艘湄公河上的美军快艇
蛤蟆镜映出刚刚缴获的钢盔和迷彩

他曾在假想的岸上跑片，两边街景
改变了向度。他曾暴走于背向观众的
银幕反面，愈益从终场的豁然大亮

回溯暗和黑，反潮流乱发混杂着藻饰
——只要他稍停，就顺势被冲走
电影院就响起另一部片子的另一支乐曲

*

那时候跑片未到，两个人中途
退场。两个人眯缝眼回避强光
散漫于整个世界的迷惘

两个人想去烟纸小店，不想
拐进了工农兵公园。小树林筛选
正午的喧响，枝条编织密秘的海

The pale billowing green spun into a star chart, and distant lyres
played on pussy and prick, afterwards they once again could hear
the solemn grief announced by the loudspeaker on the telephone pole

*

If the spinning film wasn't a nightmare, what was filmed
wouldn't be the ruins shedding another layer of skin
in the cycle of mourning, a black and white portrait

was a flag at half-mast, not bowing to the fissured earth
but reducing the freezing point in the crystal sarcophagus
until it seemed a great man's body and theories could keep fresh

until dusk, when the mood and pace of the audience at the end of the show
which still hadn't completely woken with blanking of the screen
immediately snuck into the python-camouflaged parade to celebrate

*

Some hid inside themselves to celebrate. Others
watched soft core porn to oppose the hard left, erecting their upright morality...
  others
withdrew from the public square of liberalism

unleashing their anarchic instincts on the dictatorship
of their organs night after night. And when memory also announced its
  withdrawal
did others start up a song of happiness? Did others hurriedly

send secret messages to the future? He and she would meet again
in the big marriage marketplace in People's Park
where they'd try to find a match for their children

*

Now, the shocks and aftershocks of what's left of life shake
most of the theater's towering decadence. The weighed-down sky
is still traversed by satellites, orienting the broadcasts

波涛嫩绿翻卷星图，天琴渺远
奏弄屄屌。完事后两个人又能听见
水泥电杆上喇叭广播庄严的沉痛

*

盘旋的胶片要不是噩梦，其中所摄
就不是废墟蜕开又一层蛇皮
哀悼周里，一面黑白影像的

半旗，未朝迸裂的大地鞠躬
但却下降了水晶棺里的冰点刻度
直到仿佛，伟人的身体和主义被保鲜

直到黄昏，观众散场的意绪和步伐
还没有因为刚刚变空的银幕而全醒
即刻就混进巨蟒迷彩的游行去狂欢

*

另有人躲到自我里狂欢。另有人
看毛片，背叛毛思想，勃然雄起了
德育导师……另有人撤离自由化广场

将无政府本能，放浪于器官的
一夜夜集权。而当记忆也告撤离
另有人从头越唱起谋幸福？另有人赶紧

私通未来？他和她再相会
在工农兵公园的婚姻大卖场
款睇款情，各自奏弄自家的儿女

*

现在，撼及余生的余震又摇晃
大半座电影院屹立的颓废。压低的天空
依然掠过人造卫星，定位着广播

of emotion culled by tearful scenes…the half-mast flag
has been raised to the highest, turning
the earth's overturned turned-over image. The film-runner is still

bound up in the depths of old movies, crying for help in secret
film caches with his dying breaths
now, the last shocks come from the quivering of historical records

*

A thousand kilometers away, and a thousand and one days. The two
are naked, slipping out of their bodies into a new home movie theater
they look back in the high resolution of the liquid crystal screen

The same two people, gasping for a future here and now
the same two people in each other's stage narration, and as before
they darken each other's days, starting up the motors of their bodies' desires

like tourist speedboats on the Mekong. Maybe they are
on the riverbank, pussy and prick wet with the watery screen of
their own soft core film…and like before they are in the market for a match

Translated by Eleanor Goodman

泪眼镜头筛选的感动……半旗
现在被扬到了最高位置，去翻卷
大地翻覆的翻身形象。跑片人依然

缠绕在无数旧胶片深处，从密秘
片库里，他奄奄一息的最后呼救
现在，总算撼及，源自历史纪录的震颤

*

一千公里外，又一千零一日。两个人
赤裸，褪身于新买的家庭影院
两个人回头看，液晶宽屏的高清镜子里

照样有两个人，喘吁未来的此时此地
照样有两个人相互暗场，照样各就
彼此的黑昼，发动身体如欲望摩托

像湄公河上的旅游快艇。或许两个人
恰在河上，任流水银幕打湿了屄屌
自我的毛片里……两个人照样款睇款情

Chen Li (陳黎)

In a City Alarmed by a Series of Earthquakes

In a city alarmed by a series of earthquakes, I hear
a thousand black-hearted jackals say to their children,
"Mama, I was wrong."
I hear the judge cry
and the priest confess. I hear
handcuffs fly out of newspapers, blackboards drop into cesspools. I hear
writers put down their hoes, farmers take off their glasses,
and fat businessmen strip off their clothes of cream and balsam.

In a city alarmed by a series of earthquakes,
I see madams on their knees return vaginas to their daughters.

Translated by Chang Fen-ling

在一個被連續地震所驚嚇的城市

在一個被連續地震所驚嚇的城市，我聽到
一千隻壞心的胡狼對他們的孩子說
「媽媽，我錯了。」
我聽到法官哭泣
牧師懺悔，聽到
手銬飛出報紙，黑板掉落糞坑，聽到
文人放下鋤頭，農人放下眼鏡
肥胖的商人逐件脫掉奶油跟膏藥的衣裳

在一個被連續地震所驚嚇的城市
我看到老鴇們跪著把陰戶交還給它們的女兒

The Love Song of Buffet the Clown

Simply because half the world's sorrow rests on the bridge of his nose,
Buffet the Clown stays awake the whole night. He laughs,
radiating light as dutifully as a street lamp.
No other machine is more awkward; he hangs a hammer on his chest
to guard, to watch over time,
as if his hands rather than his legs were the clock hands of infantile paralysis.
Our righteous Buffet knows no hunger.
He lives frugally, keeping his figure slim for the numerous affectionate ladies on the balcony.
His hat is a paint-chipped weathercock,
chasing the dandruff of dreams day and night.
His eyelashes are the illegitimate children of pelicans,
his sighs the female cousins of crows.
But how proud the neck covered with lipstick marks,
persisting in its slenderness more gracefully than a giraffe.

Simply because half the world's happiness rests on the bridge of his nose,
Buffet the Clown stays awake the whole night.
He laughs, he laughs, behind the eyes sour and yellow as lemons.
For the tiny eyedrops of love
he must cry, must pretend to cry sadly.
No more honest magic can ever be seen.
He presses a curved glass wand close to his ears
to turn the evil curse into grape juice and make it flow into his mouth.
But you must forgive his speeding heartbeat;
timid Buffet is at best half a great ropewalker,
dancing shakily before the slanting electric guitars.
Ah, when the ladies and the stars fall out of love,
Buffet the Clown reads the moonlight
and imitates a broken clockwork orange, singing silently.

Simply because half the world's superiority rests on the bridge of his nose,
Buffet the Clown stays awake the whole night.
He cries, he laughs, in the upside-down dressing mirror.
For the sake of the ladies' bright spirits
he adorns carefully, rubs laboriously
and polishes his wits as if they were worn-out shoes.
And without his knowledge dust moves into his hair,

小丑畢費的戀歌

僅僅因為半個世界的悲哀都枕在鼻樑
小丑畢費一夜不能睡。他笑
路燈一樣盡責的發光
再沒有更笨拙的機械了，他把一隻鐵槌掛在胸前
警戒，警戒著時間
彷彿手比腳更應該是小兒麻痺的指針
我們正直的畢費他不知道饑餓
節衣縮食，為包廂裡諸多愛他的仕女保持苗條的身段
他的帽子是掉了漆的一隻風信雞
日夜不停地追逐夢的頭皮屑
他的睫毛是鵪鶉的私生子
他的嘆息是烏鴉的表姊妹
但多驕傲啊，那印滿唇膏的脖子
比一隻長頸鹿更優雅地堅持它的纖細

僅僅因為半個世界的快樂都枕在鼻樑
小丑畢費一夜不能睡
他笑，他笑，在檸檬一般酸黃的眼睛後面
那是為了小小的愛的眼藥水
他必須哭泣，必須假裝傷心的哭泣
再見不到更誠實的魔術了
他把彎彎曲曲的玻璃棒貼在耳邊
讓惡毒的詛咒變做葡萄汁流進嘴裡
但原諒他逐漸加快的心跳
怯弱的畢費至多只是一半的大走索者
面對歪歪斜斜的電氣吉他顫抖顫抖地舞蹈
啊，那是當仕女們跟星星都失戀的時候
小丑畢費讀著月光
學一只斷了發條的桔子，無言歌唱

僅僅因為半個世界的優越都枕在鼻樑
小丑畢費一夜不能睡
他哭，他笑，在顛倒的化妝鏡中
那是為了仕女們明亮的心情
他小心地修飾，辛苦地摩擦
像對待一雙破了又破的皮鞋般擦亮他的機智
而塵埃偷偷住進他的髮間

wrinkles of desire crawl up his babyish face like a giant spider…
Ah, Buffet the Clown has no mask.
Buffet the Clown has no Oedipus complex.
He must anger, must get jealous,
must write love poems on every disposable handout like a forgotten hero,
and on the glorious morning—
march into the printing house of sunshine with all the vermiform appendixes in the city.

Translated by Chang Fen-ling

慾望的皺紋像一隻大蜘蛛爬在他嬰兒的臉上……
啊，小丑畢費沒有面具
小丑畢費沒有戀母情結
他必須憤怒，必須嫉妒
必須像湮沒的英雄把情詩寫在每一張順手見棄的廣告單上
在偉大的清晨——
跟著全城的盲腸一起走進陽光的印刷場

A Vending Machine for Nostalgic Nihilists

Please make a selection
Mother's milk • cold • hot
Drifting cloud • large packet • medium packet • small packet
Cotton candy • instant • enduring • tangled
Daydream • canned • bottled • aluminum foil
Charcoal roasted coffee • with homesickness • with passion • with death
Star perfume • with chirping of insects • with twittering of birds • original
Sleeping pill • vegetarian • non-vegetarian
Misty poetry • two pieces in one • three pieces in one • aerosol
Marijuana • *Freedom* brand • *Peace* brand • *Opium War* brand
Condom • commercial use • noncommercial use
Shadow facial tissue • extra-thin • transparent • water-proof
Moonlight ball pen • gray • black • white

Translated by Chang Fen-ling

為懷舊的虛無主義者而設的販賣機

請選擇按鍵

母奶 ●冷 ●熱
浮雲 ●大包 ●中包 ●小包
棉花糖 ●即溶型 ●持久型 ●纏綿型
白日夢 ●罐裝 ●瓶裝 ●鋁箔裝
炭燒咖啡 ●加鄉愁 ●加激情 ●加死亡
明星花露水 ●附蟲鳴 ●附鳥叫 ●原味
安眠藥 ●素食 ●非素食
朦朧詩 ●兩片裝 ●三片裝 ●噴氣式
大麻 ●自由牌 ●和平牌 ●鴉片戰爭牌
保險套 ●商業用 ●非商業用
陰影面紙 ●超薄型 ●透明型 ●防水型
月光原子筆 ●灰色 ●黑色 ●白色

Chen Li (陳黎)

In the Corners of Our Lives

Many poems live in the corners of our lives.
They may not have reported to the domiciliary registration office
or received doorplate numbers from the police station.
Walking out of the alley, you bump into a jogger speaking on flip phone.
His embarrassed smile reminds you of the old doctor who polishes his
young wife's red sports car in front of the house every night.
You realize then that they are two stanzas of a long poem.

Objects are known to each other, but don't drop in for tea.
Some float up to become images, courting and showing affection
for others. Sound and smell usually conspire first, flirting with each other
on the sly. Colors are the coy little sisters who must stay home,
get ready the curtain, sheet, bathrobe and tablecloth, wait for their master to return, and turn on
the lights. A poem, like a home, is a sweet burden
sheltering love and lust, suffering and sorrow, taking in the good and the bad.

They needn't go to the health center to be sterilized or to buy condoms
though they have their own ethics and family planning.
Couples of well-matched family backgrounds do not always make the best matches.
Of course water mixes well with milk, but it can also mate with fire.
Whitehead eats black-boned chicken; black-headed flies debate
whether a white horse is a horse. Tender violence.
Deafening silence.
Incestuous love is poetic license.

Some of them choose to live in the shadow of metaphor or the forest of symbols.
Some are broad-minded and optimistic, like sunny spiders climbing here and there. Some
enjoy living outdoors, talking idly and having intercourse; others, like invisible yarn,
are scattered in your brain, which is divided into many small suites for rent, from time to time
switching on the spinning wheel of dreams or subconsciousness.
Many poems are said to be imprisoned in the room of habit. In quest of lines you
close the door, overturn boxes and cupboards, call out desperately, and even ride an electronic donkey,

在我們生活的角落

在我們生活的角落住著許多詩
它們也許沒有向戶政事務所申報戶口
或者領到一個門牌，從區公所或派出所
走出巷口，你撞到一位邊跑邊打大哥大的慢跑選手
尷尬的笑容讓你想到每天晚上在家門前幫年輕太太
擦紅色跑車的老醫生，原來
它們是一首長詩的兩個段落

物件和物件相聞而不必相往來
一些浮升成為意象，向另一些意象
求歡示好。聲音和氣味往往勾搭在先，暗自互通
聲息。顏色是羞怯的小姊妹，它們必須待在家裡
擺設好窗簾床罩浴袍桌巾，等男主人回家，扭開
燈。一首詩，如一個家，是甜蜜的負擔
收留愛慾苦愁，包容肖與不肖

它們不需到衛生所結紮或購買避孕套
雖然它們也有它們的倫理道德和家庭計畫
門當戶對不見得是最好的匹配
水乳固然可以交融，水火也可以交歡
黑格爾吃白斬雞，黑頭蒼蠅辯論
白馬非馬。溫柔的強暴
震耳欲聾的寂靜
不倫之戀是詩的特權

它們有的選擇活在暗喻的陰影或象徵的樹林裡
有的開朗樂觀，像陽光的蜘蛛四處攀爬。有些
喜歡餐風飲露清談野合，有些則像隱形的紗
散佈在分成許多小套房出租的你的腦中，不時
開動夢或潛意識的紡織機
許多詩據說被囚禁在習慣的房間。你閉門
覓句，翻箱倒櫃，苦苦呼喚，甚至騎著電子驢

drive the mouse and pound the keys. You open the window
to the big wide world, and surprisingly, there they are:
Irises after the rain. A flock of gulls
on their way home from school. Slanting
waves of the ocean.
The microwave oven boiling tomato soup with slices of bean curd.

It occurs to you to buy some peas. You go to the supermarket and see
cancancancancancancancancancancancancancancancancancan
cancancancancancancancancancancancancancancancancancan
cancancancancancancancancancancancancancancancancancan
You grab one and find what you've been racking
your brains for owes its presence to its absence:
cancancancancancancancancancancancancancancancancancan
cancancancancancancancan   cancancancancancancancan
cancancancancancancancancancancancancancancancancancan

A persimmon lies solitary on the counter. You say,
how fantastic, a persimmon lies solitary on the counter.
A line of words forms a family in itself.
You can't help but suspect it immigrated from Japan, or from the High Tang,
when quatrains were flourishing.
But you don't mind at all. You don't mind at all that they'll all fit into
a small shopping bag.

Translated by Chang Fen-ling

驅趕滑鼠，敲鍵搜尋。打開窗戶
寬天厚地，它們居然在那裡：
雨後的鳶尾花。放學回家的
一隊鷗鳥。歪斜的
海的波紋
煮著一鍋番茄和幾片豆腐的微波爐

你想到還要幾粒豌豆。你走進超市看到
罐頭罐頭罐頭罐頭罐頭罐頭罐頭罐頭罐頭
罐頭罐頭罐頭罐頭罐頭罐頭罐頭罐頭罐頭
罐頭罐頭罐頭罐頭罐頭罐頭罐頭罐頭罐頭
你隨手拿了一罐，發現挖空心思，刻意
求索的它，原來因缺席而存在：
罐頭罐頭罐頭罐頭罐頭罐頭罐頭罐頭罐頭
罐頭罐頭罐頭罐頭　　罐頭罐頭罐頭罐頭
罐頭罐頭罐頭罐頭罐頭罐頭罐頭罐頭罐頭

一顆紅柿孤獨地在收銀台上。你說
妙哉，一顆紅柿孤獨地在收銀台上
一行字自成一戶
你不免懷疑它移民自日本或多絕句的盛唐
但是你完全不在意。完全不在意它們可以全部裝進
一個小小的購物袋

Che Qianzi (车前子)

Magnificent

She has a hat of zoo on her head,
senses the ground will tremble.
(I rented housing at the buffalo's back, a bit far from home,
water buffalo, lean as a few bones wrapped in newspaper.

And fat sheep,
wool plucked clean,
only the size of frogs.
Hands joined to pull the sailboat along the river bed

into the kitchen for firewood.
Sampan as small as a dark female animal
can only seat one dick to cross the ocean for study abroad.
In winter she staggers, ahead of summer

green group whirlpool (turn around, regret saluting the acquiescent crowd,
he raises mules to hand over to Jesus living upstairs,
brush teeth, "belch out smoke non-stop,"
two women share one breast

to feed their children, scuffle in the doorway,
tuffs of blonde hair swirl around on the ground,
secrets, so that the little girl's purity, by the hand of God,
touches the little boy's comma,

roaring church in the car. Surrounding the drive-in church
are fields of grain, wild boars the day before yesterday
shot to death like people. In solitude is a kind of relaxation and forbearance,
everyday the blood of wild boars saws off grain leaves.

Translated by Jia Yun & Jeff Twitchell-Waas

壮丽

她戴着一顶动物园在头上，
感觉地面会震动。
（我在水牛背租房，离家有点远，
水牛，瘦得像用一张报纸包起的几根骨头。

而肥胖绵羊，
把毛拔掉，
也就青蛙大小。
齐心协力，把河床上的帆船，

拖到厨房当柴烧。
舢舨小如玄牝，
只能坐进一根鸡巴漂洋过海去留学。
冬天她步履蹒跚，比夏天提前，

绿群的漩涡（回头，悔过从众的行礼，
他举起骡子递给住在楼上的耶稣，
刷牙，“不停地往外喷烟”，
两个女人共用一只乳房，

为喂自己孩子，门口打架，
扯落在地的金发团团转，
隐私，那么小女孩的纯洁是用上帝之手，
碰碰小男孩逗号，

汽车里轰鸣的教堂。汽车教堂周围，
是片麦田，前天有只野猪，
被枪像人一样打死。孤独中有种悠闲与认命，
野猪血一天天锯断麦叶。

Che Qianzi (车前子)

Southern Clown 1

Air force pillow, go,
go to the Forbidden City and sleep.
A small unit of cavalry took a shortcut,
occupies the exhibition period
court painter of scattered birds and beasts,
after bearing shadows[1]
concealed Garden of Myriad Beasts. Copulative
history, black night give me critics
and a critic as wife

——

A thin thin book,
a papa's hooves,
just as chicken feet,
someone screams pleasantly

——

My genitals
tossed in the vegetable patch,
might just be a head of endive.

Translated by Jia Yun & Jeff Twitchell-Waas

[1] The phrase is ambiguous. Grouping the characters differently might mean "take along the movie queen." Che Qianzi's work is notable for these divergences.

南方丑角 1

空军枕头，去，
去故宫，睡。
一小队骑兵走了捷径，
占领展期，
鸟兽散的宫廷画师，
携影后，
深藏万牲园。交媾的
历史，黑夜给我评论家
和评论家太太。

——

一本薄薄的书，
一只爸爸的蹄，
像如鸡爪，
有人叫得好听。

——

我的性器，
丢在菜地，
就能是棵莴苣。

Che Qianzi (车前子)

Nature of Water

Withered grass assembles in silence,
too much, know too much of dust,
plans for a memoir?
fresh grass assembles in the doorway.

The tip wants to crawl up into the body,
east of the tongue enters green fields of sugarcane,
section by section the stick passes upward,
like an adult nursery:

resurrection is vengeance on children,
in a flash a box of matches lights, gorgeous
headshot, wiser air drifts to taste,
southern clowns in every flavor,

and tends to thunderous fury!
Trembling thread will be woven into alarming brocade garments,
collapse, a past life passing through,
passed through: storm-swallows,

two black legs carried into the street,
exposing an insipid triangle of scorn,
between deciphered branches sways an answering helmet,
old society without a single merit.

Discover tea brown, from oneself,
concentrated like midnight light,
now the emptied stage lips pressing tight,
slowly reluctant to set out, the owl,

rascals temporarily break from everyday costs,
causes you to praise the red-letter window.
"Across the countryside, talking in the iris dung pile:
raised hand, lost in the sky."

水性

枯草集合于寂静，
太多了，知道太多尘埃，
有没有回忆录打算？
青草集合于门口。

尖顶在体内要往上爬，
舌头以东进入青绿的甘蔗田，
一节节棍子往上递送，
像成年苗圃：

复活是对儿童复仇，
瞬间划亮一盒火柴，爆头的
华丽，开窍的空气流于味觉，
南方丑角五味俱全，

而偏于雷霆震怒！
抖线会织成惊心锦衣，
虚脱总有一件前世穿过，
穿过了：暴雨燕子，

两条黑腿抬到大街，
露出寡淡的三角蔑视，
破解的树枝间晃动答案头盔，
旧社会一无是处。

发现茶色，从自己，
浓得仿佛午夜之灯，
现在散场的舞台双唇紧逼，
迟迟不愿启程，猫头鹰，

暂时摆脱开销日常的鼠辈，
使你赞美窗户红字。
“隔着田园，鸢尾粪堆中交谈：
举起的手，在天空迷路。”

Che Qianzi (车前子)

The aged voice you are,
nothing lacking, except youth.
Next meeting will be war games:
photo-tigers chase the fleeing all over the city—

gold leopard. I'm so glad to hear news,
crowded like Dalmatians at the lost and found.
Depressed now and then, dappled paws step on recordings,
photo-tigers chase recording women,

(the tape rewinds to dust: it has the nature of water.

Translated by Jia Yun & Jeff Twitchell-Waas

苍老的声音你在，
什么都不会缺，除了青春。
下次见面将是游戏战：
照片虎追逐城里四处逃窜的——

金钱豹。我很高兴听到消息，
密集如失物招领处的斑点狗。
有时是抑郁的，花爪踩住录音，
照片虎追逐录音女，

（磁带倒回尘埃：它有水性。

Che Qianzi (车前子)

Southern Clown 2

Talking, turns around slowly,
his whiskers imposing, who plays the tyrant?
Whom did the tyrant play?
Bulls play cows, borrowing nipples from ants.

Angels play demons,
taking their figures from bare-boned lone swine.
Demons can't be bothered to play,
carry on as demons.

Talking by the riverside,
straight demon, frank demon,
no beating round the bush,
absolutely fearless,

underrated nasal sound quite serious, just over a cold.
"Prior to opening the mouth ignorant and incompetent . . ."
yet another detail,
with difficulty, the little box produces a retroflex sound.

Translated by Jia Yun & Jeff Twitchell-Waas

南方丑角 2

说着话，缓缓转身，
他的胡子威严，谁扮暴君？
暴君又扮了谁？
公牛扮奶牛，向蚂蚁借乳头。

天使扮魔鬼，
借身材，向瘦骨伶仃的猪。
魔鬼没什么想扮，
继续魔鬼。

在河边说着话，
魔鬼直接，魔鬼坦率，
只有它不拐弯抹角，
能够无所畏惧，

低估的鼻音很重，感冒刚好。
“开口之前不学无术……”
还有一个细节，
艰难地，匣子发出卷舌音。

Southern Clown 3

Also excessively sensationalizing these breasts,
one sharpening pencil after another,
maintain productive tension and length.
Let animals,

turn into animals of interwoven muscle,
high drunk on the bank of the water tower,
palm trees yet to be used,
grab a mirror to smash—

every three steps, there's a fragment cop checking scripts:
they know about difficult writers,
scribble and revise,
looks like pubic hair, actually it's a map:

(these "Southern Clowns" anytime any place,
tug-of-war on the Boulevard of Eternal Peace, playmates soulmates,
debate blowing up the Arc de Triomphe.
Signs encountering hot water rapidly swell.

Translated by Jia Yun & Jeff Twitchell-Waas

南方丑角 3

也太耸人听闻这些乳房，
一支支铅笔削尖，
保持出厂的紧张感与长度。
让动物，

变成肌肉编成的动物，
水塔岸上喝高，
还没使用的棕榈树，
拿面镜子打破——

每走三步，就有一个碎片警察检查手稿：
他们知道困难的作家，
涂涂改改，
看上去阴毛，其实是幅地图：

（这些古今中外的“南方丑角”，
在长安街拔河，两小无猜，
共商炸掉凯旋门。
符号遇到热水膨胀迅速。

Gao Xing (高兴)

Water Bird

Out of the blue,
a streaked obstacle
springs to the surface.
Or is it a shadow of the sky?

The water bird, blinking,
swims near, taps his beak on it,
recoils. *What shall I do?*
The bird hesitates in the water,
considering its options:
turn back, dive or fly.
Three paths, three possibilities, three directions.

He turns back, swims
a few strokes, turns around again,
and suddenly dives. A moment later,
on that side, his head and neck resurface.
Then he rises into the air,
in the direction of the horizon.
The bird is certain
it can have all three choices
as if they all were one.

Only that bird is qualified to talk about freedom.
He says nothing.

There's no need for him to say anything.

Translated by Liang Yujing

水鸟

绝没有料到
水面上也会冷不丁地
冒出带着斑纹图案的障碍
这难道是天空投下的幻影？
水鸟眨了眨眼
小心翼翼地游近，用喙试了试
又赶紧缩回。该如何是好？
该如何是好？水鸟停在水中
琢磨着，迟疑着
仿佛有三条路摆在面前：
折返，潜泳，或者飞翔
三条路，三种可能，三个方向

只见那水鸟先是折返，游了
几步，随后转身，一个猛子
潜入水中，片刻之后又在
障碍的那边，露出头颈
最终奋力一搏，飞了起来
朝向天空，朝向自己所认定的
远方，将三条路变成了一条路
三种可能变成了一种可能
三个方向变成了一个方向

那水鸟才有资格谈论自由
可它却什么也没说

它已什么也不用说了

Gao Xing (高兴)

Piscine Raindrops

All at once
In a lightning flash
Raindrops turn into fish
Transparent and blue
Flapping and flopping

On the land's surface
Some people panic
They scurry off and hide
Some people are ecstatic
They spread their arms

I blink my eyes and cry out:
"Look, the sky is dreaming! The sky is dreaming!"

Translated by Denis Mair

雨，或鱼

蓦然
雷电一闪
雨变成蔚蓝、透明的鱼
纷纷扬扬落下

地球上
一些人惊慌失措
狼狈逃窜
另一些人激动不已
张开手臂

我眨眨眼，随后连声高呼：
瞧，天空在做梦！天空在做梦呢！

Gao Xing (高兴)

Farewell

Bury the beckoning cry
Bury the scenery beyond the sky
Bury my hands
Bury eyes that open on fingertips

Let time stand still on an afternoon
Let teacups and chair stay as they were
Let a perfumed lily turn about
For one last look, just that glance
Then break it all apart,
Cast it all into the sea

Days pass as always; the world is as before
Only fish will discover: at the sea bottom
There are fragments hurrying about

Translated by Denis Mair

告别

把呼唤埋葬
把天空之外的景致埋葬
把手埋葬
把手指上的眼睛埋葬

让时间停滞，在一个午后
让茶杯和椅子保留原样
让香水百合转过身来
最后望一眼，就一眼
接着，砸烂它们，将它们
扔进海里

日子依旧。世界依旧
惟有鱼发现：
海底，一些碎片正在奔走

Gao Xing (高兴)

Yueyang Tower

Ten thousand men are reciting
Their voices merging, unifying,
seizing the sky over the lake,
island after island
is nominated
emblem of the city
Only that girl
raises her head distracted
to glance at the pavilion
then quickly bows
blushing as if she committed
an unpardonable sin
Ten thousand men are reciting
ten thousand faces at that instant
are blending into One
blushing face
of that innocent girl

Translated by Liu Xuelan

岳阳楼

十万人在吟诵
声音和声音合并，统一
声音占领高空，湖面
一座座岛屿
被任命为
这座城市的形象代表
唯独那个女孩
一时走神，竟抬起头
迅速望了一眼岳阳楼
又迅速低下了头
脸颊通红，仿佛犯了
一个不可饶恕的错误
十万人在吟诵
十万张面孔，在那一瞬间
变成了一张面孔
那个脸颊通红
却无比清纯的女孩的面孔

Gao Xing (高兴)

In Memoriam

Every year the same day
pulled by an invisible hand
she would find her way to the square
walking the path again and again
from east to west, then west to east
as if to leave her footprints, then
to erase the trace; as if
to awaken the memory,
then to delete the storage;
as if she is a prompter
and a silencer,
a comma, and a full stop

Did that night ever exist?
Dizzy and weary, she couldn't help
questioning. Then
dark shadows followed
affirming her doubt
through denial, still she couldn't help
walking and walking
with no audible sound
with no visible sign
only determined to finish twenty-seven laps

Translated by Liu Xuelan

记忆

每年同一天，被某只
无形的手拖拽着
她都会来到那座广场前
从东到西，再从西往东
走了一趟，又一趟
仿佛留下足印，随即
又擦去足印；仿佛
唤醒记忆，随即又
删除记忆；仿佛这一刻
既是自己的提词员
又是自己的消音器
既要当逗号，又要做句号

那一夜真的存在过吗
疲惫和晕眩中，连她自己
都禁不住发问。这时
一个个暗影紧紧跟上
以否定的方式肯定了
她的疑问，但她自顾自
不停地走着，走着
已听不见任何声音
已看不到任何迹象
只是决意要走满二十七圈

Huang Fan (黄梵)

SONG OF THE CITY

Familiar clothes, familiar traffic
Familiar sunset in the streets
Familiar street fight, suddenly
I hate everything I see

The passing rain disinfected the city
The bad news barging in hardens middle-aged bones
It's true, life can't just be about inspecting new streets—
Looking up at a high-rise, I fear everything done in the name of my country…

Our city is vast and limitless, but what is there worth loving?
Survival has become the only landscape
Mediocrity has become our blood
We have too many slogans, and too few loves

Translated by Margaret Ross

城市之歌

熟悉的服饰，熟悉的车流
熟悉的街巷中的落日
熟悉的街头的斗殴，只一瞬
我就厌恶了眼前的一切

是一场刚结束的阵雨，打开了清新
是鲁莽闯入的坏消息，在阻止中年的钙流失
是的，生活不能只用新的街道来验收——
仰望高楼，我惊恐于什么都以祖国的名义……

我们的城市无边广大，但有什么值得我们去热爱？
活下去，成了唯一的江山
平庸，成了我们周身的血
我们的口号绰绰有余，我们的亲人寥寥无几

Huang Fan (黄梵)

NANJING NIGHT SONG

9:00
The moon grows bright black hair
and lures men like light
lures moths

10:00
Us: night's servants
putting on our sunglasses

11:00
The sound of footsteps enters a dream
and turns into sinister knocking

12:00
No one's lonelier than someone awake now—
all sleeping pills do is keep worry from exploding

1:00
A tree root kicked
and tripped a night walker

2:00
One drunk, two drunks
split by the silver axe
of the moon

3:00
A shadow on duty under the lamp
longs for a flying dream to dissolve it

4:00
Love crawls through a dream
licking wounds with dew

5:00
The Milky Way shatters, scattering handcuffs
to lock up students reading at dawn

南京夜曲

九点
月亮开始长出乌亮的长发
让男人着迷，如同灯
让蛾子着迷

十点
我们——黑夜的仆人
一同戴上它的墨镜

十一点
脚步声闯进了梦里
成为阴险的敲门声

零点
没有谁比醒着的人更孤独
安眠药，只是不让焦虑爆炸

一点
树根翘起腿来
绊倒了一个夜行者

两点
一个，两个，醉鬼
被月亮的银斧
劈倒

三点
灯下站岗的影子，多么想
被飞翔的梦蒸发

四点
在梦里爬行的爱情
用露珠舔着伤口

五点
银河开始碎成锁链
锁住了晨读的学子

Huang Fan (黄梵)

6:00
A shameless sunrise
starts to appoint its bureaucrats

Translated by Margaret Ross

六点
旭日不知羞耻
开始颁发它的委任状

Huang Fan (黄梵)

PIGEONS

I've never seen pigeons argue
I only see them soar
I don't know if a pigeon is naïve or worldly
I just know it has no past to make it toil through life

Maybe they're the tongues of the air
Lazily expressing cars' sighs
Maybe they're lined up on the roof
Vying to perform snow's wedding

One day I stick my head out the window
And realize their nation is the act of soaring
Soaring makes my silence meaningless
Thank god, they've taught me how to talk about nations!

Standing under a flock of pigeons, I think *oh*
People aren't even worth one flower blooming toward them

Translated by Margaret Ross

鸽子

从没见鸽子争吵过
只看见它们静静地飞翔
从不知，鸽子是否分天真或世故？
只知，它们没有让自己劳累一生的往事

也许它们就是空气的舌头
懒得说轿车装满的叹息
也许它们在屋脊排着队
争着当白雪结婚的司仪

直到有一天，我从窗口抬头
发现它们的祖国就是飞翔——
飞翔，让我的沉默失去了意义
谢天谢地——是它们
教会了我如何谈论祖国

当我站在鸽群下，突然觉得
人啊，甚至都比不上一朵
向鸽子仰头致意的鲜花

CHINESE AND ENGLISH

—discussing language with a friend on a winter day in Vermont

My Chinese is your coded English
for which you've lost the key.
If I talk dirty, you won't blush.

Your English is my coded Chinese.
No matter how much you say, your speech is like snow here
leading my footprints astray.

The Chinese I brought here is a song,
the lyrics are like footprints.
They say *we're winter's labels,*
which liquor bottles should we stick to?

Do you really need language to understand
the sound of a shovel digging?
I close the English book and realize
work is best weighed on untouched snow.

The snow here speaks another language.
It sows new words across a sky
filling gaps in Chinese, in English.

Translated by Margaret Ross

汉与英

——在冬日的弗蒙特，与美国友人谈语言

我的汉语，是你英语的密码
你丢了密码本
我说的粗话，已不会让你脸红

你的英语，是我汉语的密码
你说得再多，你的话也像这里的雪
让我问路的脚印，全都走错

我带来的汉语是一支歌
歌词像脚印，纷纷掉在地上
它们说，我们是冬天的标签
却不知该贴到哪种酒瓶上？

要听懂铁锹的劳动，还需要语言吗？
我合上英语课本，突然明白
没有皱纹的雪，最能称出劳动的重量

这里的大雪，说着另一种语言
它把造出的新词，撒满天空
填充着汉语和英语的空洞

Huang Fan (黄梵)

RED GRAPES

In order to see the world's evils clearly
They redden their eyes on the branch
Until they believe the warm wind's praise
In order to become waves in our blood
They offer their lives to the wine cellar

In my glass, the blood of their youth
Tries to send waves through my heart
It's a jockey riding my bloodstream
Loosening age's reins—

I used dirty words I don't normally use
Nearly scaring awake my dead relatives
I fell fast asleep with my arms around love
But, waking, couldn't find my lover

I fit right in at a banquet in the city
And finally realize, love is wine's tax
High taxes make wine noble

A crate of red wine
Is a crate of Van Goghs—do you believe that?
A crate of red grapes
Is a crate of nipples—do you believe that?

Translated by Margaret Ross

红葡萄

为了看清这世界的险恶
还在枝头，它已瞪红了眼
直到信任夏风吟唱的赞歌
为了成为血的波涛，它把一生都献给了酒窖

我的杯里，是它青春的血
试着在我心里掀起波涛
它也成了跨上我血流的骑手
一下就松开了我年龄的缰绳——

我说了平时不说的脏话
差点吓醒墓里的亲人
那一夜，我抱着爱情呼呼大睡
醒来却找不到爱人

我混迹于城市的盛宴
终于明白，爱情是红酒的税收
它用密集的税，让红酒变得高贵

一车皮的红葡萄酒
就是一车皮的凡高，你信不信？
一车皮的红葡萄
就是一车皮的乳头，你信不信？

Huang Fan (黄梵)

WHITE FACE MASK

It's like a white hand pressed over my face
After two months, I'm still not used to
Its embrace warming my sighs
Should it filter my language too?

It's a prison door for the tongue, it shuts up the ego
It won't let love get too close
It says our mouths are wounds and must be bandaged
It's like the moon, letting me bury a little wild hope in a dream

It's the most common flower blooming this spring
Trying to match the color of grief
It's also the winter inside sick lungs
It wants to freeze every face for a long time
When I complain, my mouth fills with guilt

Translated by Margaret Ross

白口罩

它像一只素手，突然捂住我的脸
已两个月，我仍不适应
它捂暖我叹息的拥抱
我说出的母语，也应该被它好好过滤？

它是舌头的牢门，关住了多少大言不惭
它让爱情，也不要靠得太近
它说我们的嘴像伤口，需要它来紧紧包扎
它像白月亮那样，让我在梦中埋下一点奢望

它是今春开得最盛的白花
试图与悲伤的颜色相称
它也是病人肺里的冬天
想在众人的脸上长久结冰
让我戴着它抱怨时，像含着满口的愧疚

Huang Fan (黄梵)

Mosquito

i flip open a book and a mosquito suddenly flies near
it sobs at me with its buzzing, confessing that i am its first love
its needlelike tongue
pumping sweet nothings into my blood

the welts on my skin itch
what did it bury inside this red grave?
the red earth on my skin expands
does it continue to excavate to give its children a proper burial?

there was a moment when we stared at each other
its stomach was bloated, obviously a pregnant female
she gave up a lithe form for the sake of her descendants
she sobs at me with her buzzing, as if to say—
please, let me go! my children will be born tonight

i put down the hand that had been tracking her movements
and like a considerate lover, endured the pain of her stings

Translated by Benjamin Landauer

蚊子

翻开书，一只蚊子突然飞来
它用嗡嗡嗡的哭声，倾述我是它的初恋？
它要用针一样的舌头
把绵绵情话注入我的血流？

我皮肤上的红包痒着
它到底把什么，埋入了这红色的坟丘？
我皮肤上的红土堆啊，越来越多
它继续挖呀掘呀，是为了掩埋它死去的孩子？

有一刻，我与它相互对望
它肚子鼓胀，分明是一个孕妇
为了子孙，它放弃了苗条的身材
它用嗡嗡嗡的哭声，仿佛说：
我今夜就要产卵，请放过我！

我放下一直跟踪它的手
开始像体贴情人那样，忍受被它咬伤的疼痛

Huang Fan (黄梵)

Hard Hat Area

is there anything good to see with these new apartment buildings?
they are our faults
what could this spat of pattering spring rain do to them?
the elder abodes crumpled to one side like gentlemen on their deathbeds
gazing at their unfilial progeny, impatiently waiting for that final breath

i step on the mud surrounding the hard hat zone
knowing that excavators are ripping away at the foundations of our fate
this city has become an eternal hard hat zone
can the incessant dust and clamor bring us happiness?
is this really the success of our labors?

suddenly, a sickly cat appears before me
to try and escape the horrors of the hard hat zone
it cries at me for quite some time, willing to sing me all sorts of songs
but i can't change anything
you'd best take me for a rock, with nothing but a countenance of pale silence

Translated by Benjamin Landauer

工地

这些新建的楼房有什么好看的？
它们就是我们身上的缺点
这场淅淅沥沥的春雨，又能把它们怎样呢？
缩在楼边的老宅子，像临死的绅士
望着不孝的儿孙，只盼着快点咽气

我踩着工地边上的泥泞
知道挖土机正在挖我们命运的地基
这座城市已成了永远的工地
永远的尘土和喧闹，还能带给我们幸福么？
这就是我们努力得到的成功么？

冷不丁，一只病猫来到跟前
为了摆脱工地造成的困境
它对我叫了很久，情愿为我唱任何歌
但我改变不了什么
就当我是一块石头吧，只有沉默的苍白的容颜

Vocabulary List

clouds, speaking in all the tongues of the world
cities, hoarding all the troubles of the world
love, embodying all the dispositions of the moon
cops, booking all the gloomy expressions of one month
morality, a public truth one cannot bear to betray in middle age, and from which can be derived wives, forced labor, and smiles
poetry, a public tomb for poets that they spend their lives renovating
dust, if you keep stirring it, who knows, you might have some luck
solitude, wherein all sounds are akin to that of a wounded bird
freedom, the emptiness you get accustomed to after forced labor
doorways, is there anything that can be insured after they've opened?
contentment, once nothing belongs to you, there's no need to worry over gains and losses
knives, the most concise way to conduct a conversation
discovery, merely speaking out the painful secrets of the ancients
dialects, some impotent clouds floating over the seas of poets' minds

Translated by Benjamin Landauer

词汇表

云，有关于这个世界的所有说法
城，囤积着这个世界的所有麻烦
爱情，体现出月亮的所有性情
警察，带走了某个月份的阴沉表情
道德，中年时不堪回首的公理，从它
　可以推导出妻子、劳役和笑容
诗歌，诗人一生都在修膳的一座公墓
灰尘，只要不停搅动，没准就会有好运
孤独，所有声音听上去都像一只受伤的鸟鸣
自由，劳役之后你无所适从的空虚
门，打开了还有什么可保险的？
满足，当没有什么属于你，就不会为得失受苦了
刀子，人与人对话最简洁的方式
发现，不过说出古人心中的难言之隐
方言，从诗人脑海里飘过的一些不生育的云

Huang Fan (黄梵)

Dancing in the Square

nobody knows me. in the june public square,
they still use dancing postures to open spring flowers
looking a little like they got attacked by insects, flailing in all directions
speakers spewing high-volume insecticide

the first time, i was as patient as a stone statue
letting the mosquitoes play freely, searching for the switch to nighttime
perhaps the gaze i gave the dancers was truly the cold stare of a stone statue
but the footsteps of my heartbeat were already in time with theirs

a lot of people wish they would stop, just stop
then, stepping on their roads home,
opening their televisions, letting the announcers speak for them
but the dancers, still dancing where they dance
walk another road that i have never seen before

their racket, after all, is a bird's nest
that calls the lonely to return home
their postures are flowery cloth
covering up the cruelty of years

i, after all, had taken my razor vision and slashed them with it daily
yet they kept on twirling, kept on dancing

Translated by Benjamin Landauer

广场舞

没有人认识我。在六月的广场
她们依旧用舞姿开着春花
还像遇到了虫害，竭力向四周
播撒高音的杀虫剂

我第一次，有了石像的耐心
任由蚊子在我身上，摸索黑夜的开关
也许我投向她们的，还是石像的冷眼
但我心里的步伐，已与她们完全一致

不少人希望她们停下，停下
踏上各自回家的路
打开电视，让播音员替她们说话
但她们，原地踏步
走着另一条我未曾看见的路——

原来，她们的喧嚣是鸟巢
吸引孤寂的人归巢
她们的舞姿也是花衣裳
帮她们遮掩岁月的残酷和沧桑

原来，我把目光的刀，天天刺向她们
她们却嘶鸣成曲，扭动成舞

Huang Lihai (黄礼孩)

Last Year in North Korea

At night, we felt our way into the hotel, one for foreign guests, inhabited by Chinese and Russians.
A solitary villa, only one TV channel with no live news
followed by patriotic war movies, a time when conquerors needed the shadow of war
to fill the silent night. We stepped into the yard, the crescent moon was faintly shining, the wind blowing over a stretch of low thatches.
Faint sounds flickered like farewells. An owl's vigilant eyes flashed in the night
We were warned not to stray far from the hotel. There was no path to the church, or to any pub.
Restless scent floating in the air of this unknown world, behind a veil,
misty sky, both the stars and the noon colorless over a lonely landscape. Trees hesitate presenting a fake truth in the wind,
Bearing in themselves a sense of fear, transformed in a flash into iron sheet. This rusty night was dark doubt itself.
We heard the waves, breath of rose in the distance, which thrilled us. The sea, you, on a stray planet,
the sad tides deep like darkness. The sea in North Korea is a caged beast, in this moment a delicate feather
However self-imposed the exile, the sea will sing its songs, time's patient enough to wait till the sea turns heart-breaking blue.
Songs enclosed in a shell will utter human voices, filling mountains and seas.

Translated by Yang Yujun

去年在朝鲜

夜晚，我们摸黑住进宾馆，一个外宾的居住地，住着中国人、俄罗斯人
此地，一个孤立的别墅，一个频道的电视，所播的新闻看不到现场
之后是爱国战争片，统治者的时间需要战争的影子来填满
寂静之夜，我们步出庭院。上弦月淡淡的照着，风吹大片低矮的茅草
一些隐隐约约的声音像告别一般明灭。猫头鹰在夜色里闪烁警惕的眼
在出去前，我们被告知不要走远。这里没有通往教堂的道，也没有去酒吧的路
夜色里飘着不安的气味，这个不为人知道的国度，一味披着神秘的面纱
苍茫的天空下，星月黯淡，照着孤独的山河。树林犹豫着，在风中展示一个假冒的真理
它的个性里却有着一丝的恐惧，瞬间变成铁片。这生锈的夜晚是漆黑的疑虑
远远的，我们听到大海的涛声，玫瑰的气息，我们兴奋起来。大海，你这迷路的行星
那悲伤的潮水深沉宛如黑色。大海在朝鲜是一头困兽。但此时它是大自然轻盈的羽毛
一个再自闭的地方，大海也要唱出它的歌，时间有足够的耐心等到海水蓝得心碎
封闭在贝壳里的歌声也要唱出人性的嗓音，充满群山和海洋

Huang Lihai (黄礼孩)

The Telescope of Barcelona

There's a telescope in the poetry of Barcelona
To see architecture, paintings, movies, music and soccer
Intertwined and yet scattered like islands
A Barcelona sky even Gaudi wouldn't weave
June markets stretch to the Mediterranean
Sea wind embraces maids' scented plaits
I swim between like a fish, seek pleasure in others' leisure
So bright and radiant, exquisite like annotations

What's handed me this telescope is an art gallery
Powerful enough to peek into the past and future
The heard and seen retreat to the depths
Repeating the murmurs of different eras
The rays of daylight raise up a pine tree like sea wind
The scent it gives off means everything and nothing as well

Translated by Yang Yujun

巴塞罗那的望远镜

巴塞罗那的诗歌里有望远镜
看见建筑、绘画、电影、音乐、足球
它们交织在一起，又像群岛散开
一个高迪编织不了整个巴塞罗那的天空
六月的市集延伸向地中海
海风拥抱姑娘芬芳的发辫
如一尾鱼，我游在其间，借别人的自由时光
寻欢作乐一回，如此明媚，像附文一般精致

递给我望远镜的是美术馆
它威力强大，窥见过去，也去往未来
被聆听和观看的退至深处
持续着不同世纪的低语
那天的光线如海风扶起一棵松树
它散发的味道，是一切又什么都不是

Huang Lihai (黄礼孩)

Radiating Jacaranda

A chance to relate my memories of Portugal
Jacaranda in the wind of Lisbon
Whose echoes have never been chained

Jacaranda is an instrument in a tree chorus
Go down a street of East Panzhihua in your hometown
Turn left and burning blue trees rush into your pupils
Blue violet reminds me of the Madonna's robe
Stepping down the stairs, with petals falling
On the piano-key steps, wind spreads petals' fingers
Sliding up and down, virtuoso vibrato extended
like a melody from heaven's concert hall

Elevated fragrance floats across your crystal eyes
I'm sketching, purple light rising from my pen
Tempted to use time as my alibi
Standing at the end of April, I'm rid of the confusion of geography
What I've longed for is not Lisbon
But you, the radiating jacaranda on that street corner

Translated by Yang Yujun

发光的蓝花楹

偶然之机，与你谈起葡萄牙的记忆
说起里斯本风中的蓝花楹
它有着不曾囚禁的回声

蓝花楹是一部合唱的树乐器
从你家乡攀枝花东区沿着街道向前
左拐，一树树蓝色的燃烧直奔眼底
那蓝紫好像圣母玛利亚的长袍
走下台阶，掉下来的花瓣，落在
琴键的台阶上，风使花瓣伸出自然的手指
上下滑动演奏，美妙的颤音延长了
天堂音乐厅送来的曲子

高处的芬芳从你清透的眼睛里飘过
我画着草图，紫色的光从笔触中跃出
这一切多像时间不在场的诱惑呀
站在四月的尽头，我摆脱了地理的困扰
原来我所顾念的，不是里斯本
而是你，那株城市转角处发光的蓝花楹

Huang Lihai (黄礼孩)

Exchanging Secrets

The sun turns back, rustling
Cools down, wind torturing wind
Bird tracks open, then fade
The same night, flowers disappear, leaving a pale void

The city's dyed, depth fades our solitude
Don't drive out the last silence to wait for a cup of coffee
At least fine weather is with us now

Chat with an appropriate match
As the world gets duller day by day, we shrink
Into two seeds in a pod
Rising toward the overlook of spring
Every moment is filled with something

Translated by Yang Yujun

交换秘密

阳光背过身去，窸窸窣窣
轻，变冷，熄灭，风折磨着风
鸟迹在弥合中带来新的裂痕
是夜，花朵失踪，留下苍白的空旷

城市被皴染，深邃使孤独变得暗淡
不要去驱赶最后的寂寞，去等到一杯咖啡
至少好天气在我们这一边

与爱得相宜的人交谈
世界日益无趣时，我们变小
成为两颗紧挨着的种子
在春天俯视的目光里上升
每一个瞬间都被什么填满

Huang Lihai (黄礼孩)

What's Shaping Us

Revolution museum on the left, bright church on the right
Now, you cross the ripples like a fish
Memory wetter than waves, shameful days in history
Can't be deleted, nobody's willing to stay disgraced

Shamian jammed with visitors seems to be a mistake
Wedding photos plastered everywhere never rectify humdrum love

Great love won't be born in pleasant weather
A man embracing dawn enters the church, mercy at heart emerges abruptly
Deeper than bright leaves overhead

Your promised land, what's shaping us
Stand by the lake of white swans, gazing in silence,
Light suspended in your heart falls on my heavy flesh
I stare, not intending to break such a spell

Translated by Yang Yujun

有什么在塑造着我们

左边革命展览馆，右边晴朗的教堂
此刻，你鱼一般穿过水的涟漪
记忆比海浪潮湿，史册上耻辱的日子
无法删除，没有人愿意在污名之上

游人如织的沙面，似乎是一场误会
到处可见的婚纱照并不纠正爱的平淡无奇
伟大的爱情不会诞生于风和日丽
曙色入怀的人走进教堂，怜悯在内心陡然升起
比头顶上明亮的树叶还要多

你的应许之地，有什么在塑造着我们
站在白天鹅的水边，静默，凝视
你内心悬浮的光落到我沉重的肉身上
我注目着，不打算打断这瞬间的奇妙

Hu Mingming (胡茗茗)

Poem Written on Hainan Airlines Menu

Two days ago, I circled the room, sorting things to take away
from things to leave behind, all the while seeking a place to hide.
The clock was ticking.

Yesterday, I circled the garden, this time sorting
the ones that could bloom, all fake,
from the ones that couldn't, all new lovers, alien lands.
The clock was packed in the suitcase.

And now, I'm circling half the world, from East to West.
Under the pitch black body of the airplane,
the Kuril Trench and the Detroit Seamount.
One moment, I'm eating a brownie bite, and in the next,
the Mariana becomes a memory.
I am flying from the 18th to the 18th.

Tomorrow, my suitcase will grow old. It can only fit
the mist of clouds and caws of crows.
As for the bright moon of the Qin and the old homeland,[2]
they're too heavy and go unclaimed, swallowed
by the conveyor belt: dark when entering,
and spit back out, so lonely.

Translated by Daniel Tay

---

[2] Reference to the Tang Dynasty Poem "Over the Border" by Wang Changling

一首写在海航酒水单上的诗

前天，我绕着房间转圈，这是要带走的
这是可留下的，顺便藏好有用之身
钟表在嘀嗒

昨天，我围着花园继续划分
会开花的都是假的
不开花的都是新欢，是他乡
钟表装进行李箱

此刻，我围着东西半球转，漆黑的机身下
是千岛海沟与底特律海山，前一秒吃下
一口布朗尼，后一秒在马里亚纳已是回忆
我从十八号飞向十八号

明天，我的行李箱就老了，只装得动
流云和乌鸦之声，至于秦时明月和故土
它们超重，且无人认领，被传送带
被吞，进去的时候是深深
吐出来，是孤零零

Night at Lake Washington

Time "dwelt nearer to those eras in history which had attracted me."[3]
Four boys and I, in the Seattle evening rain,
after a couple bottles of tequila, our young mouths
tell old tales of the Bordered Yellow Banner, Tai Laoye, and Bada Hutong,[4]
a mashup of Peking Opera and rap in the little American courtyard.
Raccoons and elk stand transfixed in the headlights,
and we too, beneath a plate of edamame and peanuts, transfixed.

This is the last drink of 2018,
this is the poem I write at year's end.
"Our failing resistance to these attacks on our sense of worth as individuals
is the central drama of our time," Paul Bowles whispers.[5]
I worry about African Swine Fever, trade wars, masters dying one after another.
The boys say chaos is just the time to make wine.
I pick up a copy of *Walden*, and see
Thoreau's wooden paddles forge a check mark in God's cup.

Without lifting my head, I see the falling leaves suffer the pain of their descent,
and the sprites in the moss donning bronze armor.
Oh, how lovely—beetroot, avocado, chickpeas.
Oh, how quickly the new year makes the boys' wings
grow feathers bright as snow.

Translated by Daniel Tay

---

[3] Henry David Thoreau

[4] Bordered Yellow Banner is one of the Eight Banners of Manchu military and society, Tai Laoye literally means maternal great-grandfather, and Bada Hutong — the Eight Great Lanes — served as Beijing's Red Light district during the Qing Dynasty.

[5] Hu Mingming misattributes this quote to Paul Bowles. It is actually a quote from Tobias Wolff appearing in a preface to Paul Bowles' "The Sheltering Sky."

华盛顿湖之夜

时间，“再次挨紧吸引我的年代”
四个男孩儿和我，在西雅图的夜雨里
喝掉两瓶龙舌兰后，年轻的嘴巴
讲述镶黄旗、太姥爷、八大胡同的旧事
美国的小庭院里响起京剧与Rap的混搭
浣熊和麋鹿在车灯下呆立
我们，在一盘毛豆花生的底部，呆立

这是2018年的最后一口酒
这是我在岁尾写下的最后一首诗
“我们节节败退的抵抗是这个时代舞台上
最引人注目的一出戏剧”，鲍尔斯附耳上来
我忧心非洲瘟猪、贸易战和大师纷纷逝去
男孩儿说乱世正好可酿新酒
我拿起一本《瓦尔登湖》，我看到
梭罗的木桨在上帝的酒杯里划着对勾

不用抬头，落叶正经历下降之苦
苔藓里的精灵身披青铜铠甲
真好啊，甜菜根、牛油果、鹰嘴豆
真快啊，新年让男孩儿们的翅膀
生出雪亮的绒毛

Hu Mingming (胡茗茗)

At the Office

At the office, in the afternoon,
I lean over my desk,
tipsy, red-faced, short of breath.
I miss a dear one, so I catcall him,
but he's too far away, and only getting farther...

Outside the window is a phoenix tree. Atop, a wild pigeon warbles.
I so envy how it tells its sorrows in full voice—
no need to be like those unfolded newspapers,
newer each day, without a soul leafing through.

Translated by Daniel Tay

在办公室

在办公室，午后
我伏在桌上
微醺、脸红、呼吸急促
我想念一个亲人，呼唤他小哥哥
可他那么遥远，且越来越远……

窗外有梧桐，上有野鸽子鸣叫
我多么羡慕它能大声吐露悲伤
不用像摊开的报纸
每日更新却没人翻动它一下

Hu Mingming (胡茗茗)

Beijing at Quarter Past Ten

This is the last match in the room.
If the flame trembles because of my hand,
may this hasty diagnosis extinguish it.

I raise my bare arms
like Beijing at quarter past ten.
Millions of skyscrapers, conventional,
throng with expressionless eyes,
their plots without suspense—
even wild pigeons have a finale to perch on.
The pathology of the city is unclear,
counts on an MRI of warm tears.
These are the cut hairs I've left behind, and
the used tissues. Three minutes later,
the lock clicks, and everything's gone—
unless that shameful damp spot,
flowing on the right shoulder of my shirt,
is just a dewy hoof on a white cloud.

Translated by Daniel Tay

十点一刻的北京

这是房间内最后的火柴
如果火苗的颤抖，是因为我的手
拜托就让潦草的诊断将它吹走

举起空荡荡的双臂
正像十点一刻的北京
广厦万千，按部就班
目无表情的人群
有着毫无悬念的剧情
就连野鸽子也有剧终可憩
病理未明的城市
指望一场热泪的核磁共振
这是我留下的断发以及
用过的面纸巾，三分钟后
门锁一碰，荡然无迹
除非我流淌在右肩衬衣上
那一小点点，可耻的潮湿
正如白云之上，露水的马蹄

Hu Mingming (胡茗茗)

Homeland of My Own

Tomorrow, I'll turn off the power and gas,
water the flowers one last time, tell them to keep.
One last time, light incense to the Buddha,
pray he guard my home, let it keep its earthly look.

To the goldfish I sent away, may you eat well and grow plump.
To the cat I sent away, forget you once called me mama.
In my house I'll find a homeland of my own.
I'll stow my daughter in my luggage.

Flying daylight to daylight, resetting the hours,
in Seattle I flip through Beijing weather forecasts,
in Beijing I count Seattle school bells.

Translated by Daniel Tay

一个人的祖国

明天，我会关好电源与煤气
最后一次给花浇水嘱咐它们保持貌美
最后一次给佛祖敬香拜托看护我的家，
让它葆有人间烟火的模样

送出去的金鱼，愿你吃得依旧肚圆
送出的猫咪，忘记你曾叫我妈妈
我在家里安顿下我一个人的祖国
我把女儿放进了行囊

从白天飞到白天，反复计算时间
在西雅图我翻看着北京的天气预报
在北京我数着西雅图的上课铃

Yong'An Street

The #12 Bus was passing by.
It splashed mud on the junkman's face.

A dog with its tail between its legs insisted on crossing the road.
In the crosswalk, it hurried left, dashed right, its life hanging by a thread.

A fly was laying its eggs in a widow's eye.
She lived in seclusion for years, shouting the lantern man's name until she died.

Along the willowy bank, the lantern man tried to stall the sunset.
In a dark place, he sang of beautiful nothingness in full voice.

The garden had mums, many branches of apricots and plums,
and "Serenade of Peaceful Joy" facing off with "Rear-Court Blossoms."[6]

Li Shishi thrust her gold hairpin into the green bricks.[7]
Likewise, a youth in white,
tears streaming down his face,
picked up a piece of iron in front of a demolition sign.

In his heart, a bulldozer sounded a roaring boom.
Then the bulldozer, like a mountain,
hailing, punishing,
densely and darkly came.

Translated by Daniel Tay

---

[6] The two titles refer to music (Qingping Yue and Houting Hua) from the Song Dynasty, during which the city of Kaifeng, where Yong'An Street is located, was thriving.
[7] Li Shishi was a courtesan during the Song Dynasty

永安街

十二路车正在驶过
它溅起的泥浆打到拾荒者脸上

夹尾巴的狗执意要到路对面
它在车轮里左奔右突命悬一线

苍蝇正在张寡妇的眼睛里产卵
她幽居数年至死喊着提灯人的名字

提灯人在杨柳岸试图拖住落日
他在暗处大声歌唱美好的虚无

园有菊，有杏梅数枝
有清平乐对阵后庭花

前朝的李师师把金钗插进青砖
后来的白衣少年
在“拆”字面前拾起一块铁并泪流满面

后来，他内心里响起推土机的巨大的轰隆声
后来，山一样的推土机
欢呼着，宣判着
黑压压地，来了…

Awaking at Midnight in Nanchang

I awoke at midnight in Nanchang, and shockingly
discovered a black shadow smoking at the other end of the hall.
I jumped up, brushed my teeth, tidied my luggage,
then lit a cigarette in a dark place.
Maybe the shadow across the hall needed company,
or maybe it was a big thing for both of us
to welcome the chirps of early birds together.

And it was indeed quite big. At any time
we could interrupt our mutual helping and threatening—
I could draw the curtain, or he could pinch out the garrulous flame.
But life really is dull, and I have missed too many memories.
"How can you commemorate without memories?"[8]

And now at daybreak, I've secreted sufficient dopamine.
I have seen everything but the figure across the hall.

Translated by Daniel Tay

---

[8] Song lyric from "Old if Not Wild" by Li Yuchun

在南昌半夜醒来

在南昌半夜醒来惊见对面
走廊里有黑影在吸烟
我腾身坐起，洗漱，收拾行李
然后，也在暗处点起一支烟
或许，对面的黑影需要陪伴
或许，我们这样对峙着共同迎来第一声鸟鸣
是一件大事儿

这事儿的确挺大。我们随时
可以中断这场彼此的帮助与恐吓
比如我拉上窗帘，比如他掐灭不肯间断的鬼火
可人生真是乏味啊，我错过的回忆已经太多
“没有回忆怎么祭奠呢？”

此时天光大亮，我分泌了足够的多巴胺
我已经看不到对面的一切

Jiang Tao (姜涛)

suburb style

dress up a little, now you look like an estate agent
every morning, open sesame, drive your electric scooter out
life demands wide green networking
why not just let the dogs out to maul people, why not just reclaim the wasteland, plant it with veg
actually people aren't so bad, they just want to spend their spare cash and misbehave

in the days that are left, to endure is to look forward
make a little time on weekends: up into the mountains for the oxygen, picking overripe fruit
sleepless late nights: a snatch of screed scribbled in defense of your rights
even if things aren't how you want them, beneath the north window
the train for baotou is still sweet

even with all its wagons vacant, all night long
it ravages the rails—making the bedfellow
melancholy too, relentlessly fiddling in the blankets
to stick, into your delicate body, a red bloom.

Translated by Josh Stenberg

郊区作风

穿体面点儿，就能像个中介了
每个早上，打开洞穴，骑电动车冲出去
人生，需要广大绿色的人脉
那随便放狗咬人的、随处开荒种菜的
人其实不坏，就想花点闲钱撒野

剩下的日子，熬着也是盼着
周末得空：上山吸氧，采摘熟烂瓜果
深夜不睡：写写打油诗维权
即使不能如愿，北边窗户下
那些开往包头的火车还是甜蜜的

甚至空了所有车厢，一整夜地
蹂躏着铁轨——惹得枕边人
也惆怅，忙不迭在被窝里
为秀气的身子，插一朵红花。

Jiang Tao (姜涛)

the wealth of nations

searing summer, all the way west to escape the heat
the workers' new town sprawls right down to the riverside
family tyranny, ceremony
generating girls who behave habitually like cadres

only the steel blast furnace still flames day and night
twenty years ago, it wasn't there to manufacture the border-soaring fighters
just to manufacture of meat lockers
i like to watch the workers, young men and women, getting off work

in twos and threes, bearing greens and soupbones
social ideals are the old hand-in-hand
parental savings heaped conveniently in the shallow parlour
as for the one who remains

having opposed conventions, will she really be left with nowhere to go?
well, while the sky is high and the clouds sparse
tell us a little something, you who will return home covered in glory!
back then, before inflation

young love was already in vogue, idle children
could only aim too high and be quiet
going, if moved by excitement, down to the riverside to skip stones

Translated by Josh Stenberg

国富论

炎炎夏日，避暑避到了西部
工人新村蔓延到小河边
家庭的暴虐、仪式
造就女孩们普遍的干部作风

只有炼钢高炉还昼夜燃烧
20年前，不为造翱翔边境的战机
只为造储备肉类的冰箱
我喜欢看男女青工一起下班

三三两两，提了青菜和肉骨头
社会理想不过是手拉手
将父母积蓄，顺便堆进浅浅的客厅
被剩下的那一个

反礼教之后，还真的无处可去了？
那么，趁天高云淡
说点什么吧，未来衣锦还乡的你！
没有通胀的当年

早恋已经普遍，无所事事的儿童
只能好高骛远地沉默
兴之所至，或到河边丢几块碎石头

Jiang Tao (姜涛)

wilderness beach

those invisible islands, with drumbeat and gong-strike
might not be inhabited by ten thousand immortals
the crab at the banquet raises its pincers,
votes to oppose, though once dismantled,
becomes sheer gourmet packaging

two intimate people—yet they can speak about democracy
and sleep together under the a/c
the sea reaches to the window, handing you a green basin to wash your face in
in dreams their faces are dirty
like they've been lashed
beneath their bodies the sand thinly flows

the winding highway carries through the green hilltops
yet more tourists from the great nation
they take pictures, shriek, all that's missing is
a five-star flag raised on the beach
when the tide comes in it carries off a nikon camera

the whole fluttering landscape a write-off
although a few painfully trashy pre-wedding pics
have amazingly survived

Translated by Josh Stenberg

野蹟海滩

那些看不见的岛，敲锣打鼓
不见得住着十万神仙
宴会上的螃蟹，举手举脚
投出反对票，结果拆卸之后
成了美味中的纯装置性

两个亲密的人，还可以讲民主
一起睡到空调下
大海临窗，像临窗递过一只绿色脸盆
他们梦中的脸，脏脏的
仿佛遭受过鞭打
他们身子下，流出了细沙

公路辗转，却从苍翠山巅相继送来
更多大国观光客
他们拍照、尖叫，就差在海滩上
升起一面五星旗帜
潮水适时卷走一架尼康相机

一切旖旎风光报废
几张痛苦的婚前不雅照
却被意外地保留了下来

Jiang Tao (姜涛)

respect

i don't respect the system, that's alright
it seems like all my friends are the same way
but i don't respect seaweed, i don't respect those
machines of nature that keep us respiring

on the lake i wear leather shoes
in the city i learn to socialize like a cloud
i lack a bent for evil, even more i lack the courage to be good
so until evening i'm in total darkness

and can only be like a knife
swathe myself tight in a quilt to sleep, letting the body's
angles express the drops of ache.
only a few square meters remain in the world

and nothing remains in the fridge but a talking skeleton.
but there's always busybodies junking things too soon
just so the awakened class can feel less crowded
on the commute

i don't respect the minority's sacrifices
just like i don't respect the salespeople who
leave home despite heavy winds, though i respect
what they accumulate in a year

such as tiny grains of dust worn on the body
there's a style i respect
even if i don't respect the new rich relatives
in the countryside, nor their privilege.

Translated by Josh Stenberg

尊重

我不尊重制度，这没关系
所有朋友都貌似一样
但我不尊重水草，不尊重自然界里
那些维系我们呼吸的机器

我在湖泊上穿着皮鞋
在城市里，学着像云一样地社交
缺少恶的取向，更缺少善的勇气
所以到了晚间，漆黑一团

我只能像刀子一样
裹紧棉被睡觉，听任身体的
尖锐处，淌出酸痛的水滴。
这世界只剩十几个平方

这冰箱里，只剩一颗说人话的头颅。
但总有好事者提早报废
好让一个觉悟的阶级，在上班时分
看上还不至过于拥挤

我不尊重少数人的牺牲
就像我不尊重刮大风
还出门工作的推销员，但我尊重
他们将一年的积蓄

像细小的尘沙，都穿在了身上
我尊重这种风格
即便我不尊重他们在乡下
有弄权的阔亲戚。

Jiang Tao (姜涛)

prophecy or recollection

finally the buck will be passed on to a third party
for instance that made-in-china tv set in the nook
whose face, like an abdicated monarch's,
is scored with ruthless late-autumn streaks

breakfast takes place outdoors to accompany birdsong
beef luncheons must be brought back inside
the struggle lingering on the grass
distinguishes the bones off the meat from all the rest

the kids kicking the ball are like a reckless flock of seabirds
in pursuit of the bubble, invisible rain is looped
by CD's in their pupils: "if"
"perhaps" "however" "anyhow"

when the terms and dishes have been scrubbed clean
and shelved, the scenery in the caved places
is still posing questions: perhaps our bodies
are tiny little parcels, delivered here by mistake

outside the maternity hospital all roads lead to this moment
a nurse, never seen before,
holds the postal parcel and over the buzz of the rectiformer
reads that blurry address

Translated by Josh Stenberg

预言或追忆

最终，责任会被推卸给第三者
譬如角落里的国产电视机
它像一位离任后的元首
满脸深秋残忍的条纹

早餐在户外进行，伴随着鸟鸣
牛肉午餐必须搬回室内
遗留在草地上的斗争
仿佛吃剩的骨头区别于万物

踢球的孩子们，像群冒失的海鸟
追逐着泡沫，不可见的雨被一张光碟
反复播放在他们眸子里："如果"
"或许"、"然而""总之"

当词语和餐具，被洗净
放回原处，风景在塌陷的地方
仍在提出问题：或许我们的身体
是小小的邮包被误投到这里

妇产院外，条条大路通向此刻
一个素昧平生的护士
抱起了邮包，在变压器的嗡嗡声中
读出了那模糊的地址

Jiang Tao (姜涛)

peach blossoms in front of the library

peach blossoms in front of the library are fated to bloom again
to suffer insect damage and praise
like wee overdue books, one after the other
flipped to the last page by bicycle bells
lifting my eyes your face is
reflected on the window, a little more frank than in years past
but if between the leaves by happenstance the
flashy lingerie of yore were peeking through
would you still sprint off
to stand, all shame-faced, ten meters away?
"who arranged this meeting?"
the little birds perched on the coin telephones
can give no answer, and the flower god, busy socializing with honeybees,
cares even less to respond
the peach blossoms are bound to bloom, while the relevant knowledge
is just now billowing gently through the library stacks

Translated by Josh Stenberg

图书馆前的桃花

图书馆前的桃花注定又要开放
历尽虫蛀和赞美
仿佛一本本过期的小书
被自行车的铃声，翻到了最后一页
抬眼望去，你在窗子上
映出的脸，是比往年诚恳了一些
但树叶之间如果偶然露出
往事鲜艳的内衣
你还会逃开
满面羞惭站在10米开外？
“是谁安排了这次会面”
投币机上站立的小鸟儿
不能回答，花神忙于应酬蜜蜂
更不屑于回答
桃花注定开放，与此有关的知识
正在书库里轻轻澎湃

Lan Lan (藍藍)

OF COURSE YOU'LL SAY

Of course you'll say humans have nothing to be proud of. For the snake,
paths lie everywhere. Don't birds find their way through the heavens?
Or fish through a vast ocean? Beyond the village houses,
above the soybean field, see that thin mist, rising limpid blue.
Those melon rows, vegetables, hands lifting
a tumble of sweet potatoes from the earth.
When hot sun kindles corn tassels red, ripening the fragrant
Artemisia—you grab your pen,
climb to the roof of the building, search the sky's depths
for one page to hold all this
just as it is.

Translated by Diana Shi & George O'Connell

你当然可以说

你当然可以说："人没什么可自大的。对于蛇来说
到处都是路。鸟飞在空中需要路吗？
还有鱼，在大海里。"你望着楼后面的村庄
黄豆地里升起的淡淡的雾霭，蓝色的——如此清澈
瓜园，菜地，人们在土里刨出滚圆的红薯
灼热的太阳点燃了玉米的红缨子，并在蒿草上
催生浓烈的香气——你抓住笔，说着，写着
攀援到这座城市的楼顶，并在天空的深处
找到一张稿纸——能放进这一切的　正是这个样子。

Lan Lan (藍藍)

UNFINISHED JOURNEY

Midnight. A string of words roars
streaking from the dark tunnel, dim blue signal light
flashing by. A train drags its umbilicus
through the trestle, my hollow chest
still trembling beneath the sleepers, pressed tight
to the arc of sky, crushed, flattened out.
You know, I

am always this way, wobbling
up at midnight, sipping water,
sitting. Letters. In the phone a droning snowfield.
Spread across the keyboard, shipped off by my own hands. Crossing mountains,
the tips of redwoods scuffing my thirsty face,
their boughs rasping. Or on the ground
shattered ice in my eyebrows. You know, sometimes

I walk beneath the cape lilac on Weisi road, carrying green vegetables.
I shove open the door, imagining your shadow. The children squeal with joy
and rush my legs. Rain slips down the windowglass.
The house starts to shake, the glide of silent wheels
towing night's chimneysmoke. Sounds of the city hush.

Downstairs the cobbler plucks a nail from his mouth,
swings the hammer, drives hard through life's sole, no
hesitation. These junkmen
haul cartloads of scrap, pocketing small coins,
their joints strong. You know, that festival

of fragrant weeds, where we anchored,
till dawn the cuckoos calling from distant woods,
from shadowed trees. Your long lashed eyes
shutting. At my hand, a glass of cool water,
the wisps of dying coals. Standing by the window
I think: I love this world. Once,
in the cleft of a moment, I had a chance.
It steered slowly close, then turned the corner.

未完成的途中

……午夜。一行字呼啸着
冲出黑暗的隧道。幽蓝的信号灯
闪过。一列拖着脐带的火车
穿越桥梁，枕木下
我凹陷的前胸不断震颤。它紧抵
俯身降落的天空，碾平，伸展
——你知道，我

总是这样，摇晃着
在深夜起身，喝口水
坐下。信。电话线中嗡嗡的雪原。躺在
键盘上被自己的双手运走。翻山越岭
从水杉的尖顶上沉沉扫过，枝条
划破饥渴的脸。或者，贴着地面
冰碴挂上眉毛，你知道，有时

我走在纬四路的楝树下，提着青菜
推门，仿佛看到你的背影，孩子们快乐尖叫
冲过来抱着我的腿。雨从玻璃上滴落。
屋子晃动起来，轮子无声地滑行
拖着傍晚的炊烟。那时，市声压低了

楼下的钉鞋匠，取出含在嘴里的钉子
抡起铁锤，狠狠地楔进生活的鞋底，毫不
犹豫。这些拾荒的人
拉着破烂的架子车，藏起捡到的分币
粗大的骨节从未被摧毁。你知道，端午时节

蒿草浓烈的香气中，我们停靠的地方
布谷鸟从深夜一直叫到天亮，在远处的林子里
躲在树荫下面。你睫毛长长的眼睛
闭着。手边是放凉的水杯和灰烬的余烟。站在窗前，
我想：我爱这个世界。在那
裂开的缝隙里，我有过机会。
它缓缓驶来，拐了弯……

Lan Lan (藍藍)

I'm always this way. Staring forever at the screen,
a string of words leaping from darkness. A dusky field.
A miner's lamp racing backward.
Hills. Ponds. Night grinds my limbs.
Misery. Monotony. Never despair
You know, at this moment one star illuminates
my bowed head: lifting the alms-bowl for rice.
An iron arm drives the iron wheel driven by a piston
—a tongue of flame shoots up. Past the window
a hung diaper, slowly rising.

Translated by Diana Shi & George O'Connell

我总是这样。盯着荧屏，长久地
一行字跳出黑暗。黝黝的田野。矿灯飞快地向后
丘陵。水塘。夜晚从我的四肢碾过。
凄凉。单调。永不绝望
你知道，此时我低垂的额头亮起
一颗星：端着米钵。摇动铁轮的手臂
被活塞催起——火苗窜上来。一扇窗口
飘着晾晒的婴儿尿布，慢慢升高了……

Lan Lan (藍藍)

KARAMAY

For the 288 children and 37 teachers killed in the 1994 conflagration.
Across the whole city, not one monument commemorates the dead.

No tears, no tombstones,
just casual oblivion in the files.

Dear child, my child,
your mother prostrate on the earth,
hauling sorrow to her grave.
Child, the rod of flame still hammers your bent backbone,
your slender arms turned black, your smoldering hair.

Three hundred twenty-five lamps gone out.
Karamay, your town square darker than the tomb.

Upon your scorched lips, child, I set the six-petaled plum blossom,
our mouths like yours smothered caves.

As if my own daughters died, the fat official
swills black oil, bloodstains on his napkin.

Karamay, the hopeless stones of the Gobi roll and murmur.

A pitch-dark coffin in a barren land. No place
more gorged on suffering, on lies.

Translated by Diana Shi & George O'Connell

克拉玛依之夜

给在“12-8”大火中被烧死的288个孩子和37位教师。
这座城市没有一寸建筑记载这场大火中的死难者。

没有眼泪。没有石碑。
亲爱的孩子。我的孩子

只有文件中若无其事的遗忘，而
扑到在地上的母亲会一直把哀号拖进坟场

孩子，火焰的铁棒还在捶击你弯曲的脊骨
你慢慢变黑的小胳膊，你冒烟的头发

三百二十五盏将要熄灭的孤单的灯
克拉玛依，你的广场比坟墓更加黑暗

我把干枯的六瓣梅放在你烧焦的嘴唇上，孩子
我们的嘴唇同样也是被堵死的洞穴

替代我的女儿死。你的血
滴在被黑色石油喂肥的官员的餐巾上

克拉玛依，戈壁中滚滚的石头全是绝望的叫喊

一具漆黑的棺木：再没有什么地方
比这片荒凉的土地充满更多的苦难和谎言！

Lan Lan (藍藍)

ARCHANGEL

The Seine slides beside you.

A windgust blows your hat
to a village in north China
as the sun drops,
fire banked in a lime kiln.
The low river shows its smooth stones,
serene as the noon breath of cattle.

Never in this world have I met

an archangel. In human form, the wings
stay hidden. But when they open,
night rises toward starlight. How brief our lives
feeding on lichens of the real.
"Is that you?" he asks.

At *Place du Châtelet, a flash of light*
as he trades wings with evening
while a soundless river flows within.
Nearby, the tower's half ladder trembles,
retreating into clouds. Time's hourglass slows

as earth's grim scars
are mantled by his wings. Grief
weighs down a rebel's eyelids.
Ruined walls, paper scraps,
a chapter still unended.
Incompletion makes him whole, offsets
the empty Paris street. Archangel,

face dimmed by sunlight, shadowy lamps,
heavy yellow pages. He comes into focus
and the ancient grove appears. Low in the sky,
silence, then notes of a golden bell.

Translated by Diana Shi & George O'Connell

大天使

的确，塞纳河在你身边走着。

的确，一阵风把你的帽子吹到
遥远的华北村落。残阳。
那里的石灰窑已熄灭它的烈火。
河水落下，露出鹅卵石的光滑
静静地，晌午的牲口打着响鼻——

但你并未在与世界的接触中遇到过它们：

大天使。他的翅膀是人的
趋向于隐匿，当它伸展
仿佛星光带来黑夜。你寄生在
可触摸之物的青苔上，多么短暂
呵，“是你吗？”他说

在莎特莱广场，如一道光闪过
平静地，他与夜空交换翅膀
带着他内流河无声的流淌。并不遥远
临街钟楼的半截梯子微微一晃
撤回云端。沙漏突然停了——

大地在飞，丑陋的疤痕
被他的双翼抬起。这悲伤的颠覆者
垂下他的眼睑。残垣、纸屑
未画上句号的断章及一滴泪水
正是这细碎的缺失使他完整，衬托出
巴黎街道的空无。啊，大天使

他以阳光遮脸，以灯火后的阴影
以发黄的沉沉书页。他消失在明晰中
因此古老的树林出现。他沉默
而低空中金色的警报骤然被拉响——

Lan Lan (藍藍)

PONT MARIE

Beyond Pont de la Tournelle,
enough green bookstalls
for André Breton's disputations,
now locking up at dusk.

To the west, upwind,
naked poplars, *Notre Dame, Île de la Cité.*
Hydrangeas on a windowsill
lean toward the riverbank. The blue hour
flicks its skirts, admitting night,
the passages of dreams.

The bridge is best for looking down.
My hands clasp the ink-green rail, still warm
as sunset fires the high, stained glass.
Carried on the air above a darkened Seine
the roll of heavy bells.

Amid such wounding light,
all this.

Translated by Diana Shi & George O'Connell

玛丽桥 ①

先是图尔内勒滨河路，两排绿房子②
小的，盛得下布勒东们的争吵。
如今他们安静了。一把旧锁合上暮色。

往西，杨树光着身子站在风中
眺望斯德岛，“我们的女士”③
是的，还有楼房窗台上的绣球花
伸长脖子张望，河水的那边
撩起黑暗的裙裾制造着夜
为了让梦通过

而桥是用来朝下看的。栏杆漆成墨绿
伸手勒住她们温暖的腰。一截灿烂
被用来装饰玻璃画。透明
沉重。收集风中滚动的钟声

它通往圣母院（啊，那下面的流水！）。
她们——
通往擦伤自身的光明。

① 玛丽桥是越过塞纳河通往圣母院最近的桥。
② 塞纳河畔有很多出售旧书的摊点，书就放在一排排绿色的箱子里。
③ 圣母院的法语原意即“我们的女士”。

Li Shaojun (李少君)

Autumn Evening

The partridge hidden inside the Boshen temple called out dusk
By the Jinshui brook bridge, stars and a few folks appeared over the lawn
Clean and calm fragrance emerged from Osmanthus flowers
In contrast to the mundane myriad of twinkling lights from the town

The busy night life under splendor lights
Folks are cooking, eating, chatting and cleaning
Families are watching TV around the couch, a person is messaging on WeChat
Every window shows shadows of people moving about

I am standing on higher ground nearby, watching them
As if a deserted me among all these
They and I divide darkness and loneliness
They and I share moonlight and tranquility

Translated by Shelley Kristina Hu

秋夜

柏森祠堂深藏的鹧鸪呼唤出暮晚
金水溪桥边，星星们和三两闲人现身草地
桂花香浮现出散逸的清氛气质
映衬着城中万家灯火世俗气息

锦里方向，华灯闪耀，夜生活一派繁忙
人们在炒菜、吃饭、闲聊和打扫
一家人围坐沙发看电视，一个人站立阳台发微信
每一间窗户里都显出人影憧憧的充实

我站在不远处的高台上，看着他们
又仿佛自己正寂寥地置身其中
我和他们平分着夜色和孤独感
我和他们共享着月光与安谧

Li Shaojun (李少君)

Liangzhou Moon

An ancient moon
Is radiating the light of nowadays

Western wind
Has been blowing into the 21st century

Tonight, the person standing on the wall watching the moon
Not Wang Wei, not Cen Shen
Not Gao Shi
—it's me

Translated by Shelley Kristina Hu

凉州月

一轮古老的月亮
放射着今天的光芒

西域的风
一直吹到了二十一世纪

今夜，站在城墙上看月的那个人
不是王维，不是岑参
也不是高适
——是我

Li Shaojun (李少君)

Probability

On the bench at the Champs-Elysees I thought
If I keep waiting
Will my love show up

Today, I'm still thinking under a tree in my hometown
She may show up when I wait under a tree
The probability could be higher

Translated by Shelley Kristina Hu

可能性

在香榭里大街的长椅上我曾经想过
我一直等下去
会不会等来我的爱人

如今，在故乡的一棵树下我还在想
也许在树下等来爱人的
可能性要大一些

Li Shaojun (李少君)

The Time of Vanity

Nihilists in the world are rioting, gesturing
From London to New York, from Europe to the Americas
The new Prague Spring was launched at the heart of capitalism
Evolved into text messages, Twitter and Weibo uprisings
No slogans, no targets and no organization
Perform repeatedly the flash mob's roar
Only gas bottles, masks, and flesh
Runaway families run on all the streets in the city
A libido revolution of idle youth
Lurking with the impulse to rebel and the anger of being deprived

I, an Asian on a distant island
Exhausted by the battle and desperate
Turn toward the embrace of the landscape, the moon and my hometown
But I still have faint concerns in the new Great Leap Forward
Will the green mountain be relocated, will the Moon Palace be demolished
someday
And everyone's hometown seems to be going through transformation

Translated by Shelley Kristina Hu

虚无时代

虚无党在全球暴动，手势所指
从伦敦到纽约，从欧洲到美洲
新的布拉格之春在资本主义的中心发起
演变为手机短信、推特和微博的起义
没有口号，没有目标也没有组织
闪族重演呼啸而来呼啸而去的行动
只有汽油瓶、蒙面和肉体之躯
暴走族世家在全城的所有街道奔突
一场无所事事的青春的本能的力比多革命
潜伏着被剥夺的愤怒和造反的冲动

我，一个遥远的海岛上的东方人
因对世事的绝望和争斗的厌倦
转向山水、月亮和故乡的怀抱
但我也有隐隐的担心，在新的大跃进中
青山会不会被搬迁，月宫是否终有一日拆除
而每一个人的故乡，似乎都正在改造之中

Li Shaojun (李少君)

Green Jade

When the country is big, there's wiggle room
When you are small, it can be grabbed in the palm to enjoy bit by bit
As soft and warm as jade
He's maneuvering between you and the country

For one moment, it's about the national business
For another, personal affairs
When he's exhausted, you are his chest rub
When it's peaceful, you are the soft spot on his heart

Translated by Shelley Kristina Hu

碧玉

国家一大，就有回旋的余地
你一小，就可以握在手中慢慢地玩味
什么是温软如玉啊
他在国家和你之间游刃有余

一会儿是家国事大
一会儿是儿女情长
焦头烂额时，你是一帖他贴在胸口的清凉剂
安宁无事时，你是他缠绵心头的一段柔肠

Ouyang Jianghe (欧阳江河)

Picasso Paints a Bull

Over the course of the next two weeks Picasso will paint a bull.
A bull whose body seems possessed by a strange reality:
the more Picasso paints, the less there is.
"Can less"—the artist asks—"become more?"
"Right on," Picasso replies.
The critic waits to see the painter's more.

But Picasso's bull just keeps getting less and less.
The hooves are first to go—then the horns,
then the skin sheds itself like a detached retina,
revealing the joints between empty spaces.
"How less does it have to get before it becomes more?"
"That depends on the name you give to more."

The critic is confused. "Would you say that in this work
you are committing moral violence on the bovine body,
shearing off every scrap of flesh with your Mediterranean wind?"
"Don't blame the wind—look at that butcher shop
across the way. Every day I watch lovely young ladies
walk home with a few dozen pounds of his meat."

"Whose meat? The meat of the bull on your canvas?"
"Now that depends on which knife you use."
"Is this a contest between the ethics of aesthetics and the ethics of life?"
"All cut up, how'd he have energy for that?"
"And what's left over? Anything?"
"No, no spirit remains. Praise waste."

"Is your bull an act of subtraction upon the world?"
"Why not addition? I imagine that butcher is
counting his cash right now." Sure enough, the next day,
the butcher's wife comes with her life savings to buy Picasso's bull.
But all she sees is a couple lines.
"Where's the bull?" she asks, indignant.

Translated by Austin Woerner

毕加索画牛

接下来的两个星期毕加索在画牛。
那牛身上似乎有一种越画得多
也就越少的古怪现象。
“少”艺术家问，“能变成多吗？”
“一点不错，”毕加索回答说。
批评家等着看画家的多。

但那牛每天看上去都更加稀少。
先是蹄子不见了，跟着牛角没了，
然后牛皮像视网膜一样脱落，
露出空白之间的一些接榫。
“少，要少到什么地步才会多起来？”
“那要看你给多起什么名字。”

批评家感到迷惑。
“是不是你在牛身上拷打一种品质，
让地中海的风把肉体刮得零零落落？”
“不单是风在刮，瞧对面街角
那间肉铺子，花枝招展的女士们，
每天都从那儿割走几磅牛肉。”

“从牛身上，还是从你的画布上割？”
“那得看你用什么刀子。”
“是否美学和生活的伦理学在较量？”
“挨了那么多刀，哪来的力气。”
“有什么东西被剩下了？”
“不，精神从不剩下。赞美浪费吧。”

“你的牛对世界是一道减法吗？ ”
“为什么不是加法？我想那肉店老板
正在演算金钱。”第二天老板的妻子
带着毕生积蓄来买毕加索画的牛。
但她看到的只是几根简单的线条。
“牛在哪儿呢？”她感到受了冒犯。

Ouyang Jianghe (欧阳江河)

Mother, Kitchen

Where the immemorial and the instant meet, opening and distance appear.
Through the opening: a door, crack of light.
Behind the door, a kitchen.

Where the knife rises and falls, clouds gather, disperse.
A lightspeed joining of life and death, cut
in two: halves of a sun, of slowness.

Halves of a turnip.
A mother in the kitchen, a lifetime of cuts.
A cabbage cut into mountains and rivers,
a fish, cut along its leaping curves,
laid on the table
still yearning for the pond.

Summer's tofu
cut into premonitions of snow.
A potato listens to the onion-counterpoint
of the knife, dropping petals at its strokes:
self and thing, halves of nothing
at the center of time.
Where gone and here meet, the knife rises, falls.

But this mother is not holding a knife.

What she has been given is not a knife
but a few fallen leaves.
A doctor hears the autumn wind in his stethoscope.
The fish leaps over the blade from the sea
to the stars. The table is in the sky now,
the market has been crammed into the refrigerator,
and she cannot open cold time.

Translated by Austin Woerner

母亲，厨房

在万古与一瞬之间，出现了开合与渺茫。
在开合之际，出现了一道门缝。
门后面，被推开的是海阔天空。

没有手，只有推的动作。

被推开的是大地的一个厨房。
菜刀起落处，云卷云舒。
光速般合拢的生死
被切成星球的两半，慢的两半。

萝卜也切成了两半。
在厨房，母亲切了悠悠一生，
一盘凉拌三丝，切得千山万水，
一条鱼，切成逃离刀刃的样子，
端上餐桌还不肯离开池塘。

暑天的豆腐，被切出了雪意。
土豆听见了洋葱的刀法
和对位法，一种如花吐瓣的剥落，
一种时间内部的物我两空。
去留之间，刀起刀落。

但母亲手上并没有拿刀。

天使们递到母亲手上的
不是刀，是几片落叶。
医生拿着听诊器在听秋风。
深海里的秋刀鱼
越过刀锋，朝星空游去。
如今晚餐在天上，
整个菜市场被塞进冰箱，
而母亲，已无力打开冷时间。

Ouyang Jianghe (欧阳江河)

Key to Sunday

A key flashes in the Sunday morning light.
A returning traveler is locked out in the dark.
A knock on the door is always more faint than
the rasp of metal in the keyhole.
Only a dreamed address is reliable.

As I bike down a quiet street
all the headlights go out at once.
In the night sky above, a hand clenches a brake.
I hear a clink. A key has fallen to the ground.

I see a ring of keys, keys of years past
glinting in the light. I pick them up.
But where are the hands that hide behind them?
A row of closed days, ending in Saturday—
but I do not know which to unlock.

Now it is Sunday. All the doors on the street
stand open. I toss the keys away.
No need to knock. Just walk right in.
Such a crowded world, and no one at home.

Translated by Austin Woerner

星期日的钥匙

钥匙在星期日早上的阳光中晃动。
深夜归来的人回不了自己的家。
钥匙进入锁孔的声音，不像敲门声
那么遥远，梦中的地址更为可靠。

当我横穿郊外公路，所有车灯
突然熄灭。在我头上的无限星空里
有人捏住了自行车的刹把。倾斜，
一秒钟的倾斜，我听到钥匙掉在地上。

许多年前的一串钥匙在阳光中晃动。
我拾起了它，但不知它后面的手
隐匿在何处？星期六之前的所有日子
都上了锁，我不知道该打开哪一把。

现在是星期日。所有房间
全部神秘地敞开。我扔掉钥匙。
走进任何一间房屋都用不着敲门。
世界如此拥挤，屋里却空无一人。

Ouyang Jianghe (欧阳江河)

Who is Gone, and Who Remains

Dusk: the boy secrets himself in a tree-root,
eavesdropping on the innards of insects.
What he hears is not the world of insects
but the world outside: for example, innards of machines.
The setting sun turns beneath his feet like the wheel of a truck,
the boy's father drives a truck
the truck is empty
                                        parked in an empty field.
The father gets out, and the soundless beauty of the sunset strikes him dumb.
He turns off his crying cell phone, says to the boy:
all things turning at the edge of the sky
have lips, have tongues. But they speak only amongst themselves,
erecting their ears upon this speech.
                The boy, refusing to believe in the ears of things, listens to the ears
                of his heart.
In truth, he is not listening at all,
but, by not listening, he overhears
a different kind of hearing—
he invents his own deafness, and soars,
rising on mute updrafts of imagination.
Behind our everyday sunset, could there be
a miracle-world alive with voices?
Could there be another boy listening, another sun
sinking in the west?
                                    Staggering sky—
The world has fallen silent: a telephone rings on, unanswered.
Machines and insects cannot hear each other's heartbeats,
and the root has been ripped from the soil.
The boy's deafness becomes dream-vision, protocol, brogue.
The truck is broken
                                        his father buries his head under the hood
and his mother sleeps, sunset cradled in her arms, not giving a thought
to the coming of night, the arrival of old age.

Translated by Austin Woerner

谁去谁留

黄昏，那小男孩躲在一株植物里
偷听昆虫的内脏。他实际听到的
是昆虫以外的世界：比如，机器的内脏。
落日在男孩脚下滚动有如卡车轮子，
男孩的父亲是卡车司机，
卡车卸空了
　　　　停在旷野上。
父亲走到车外，被落日的一声不吭的美惊呆了。
他挂掉响个不停的行动电话，
对男孩说：天边滚动的万事万物都有嘴唇，
但它们只对物自身说话，
只在这些话上建立耳朵和词。
　　　　男孩为否定物的耳朵而偷听了内心的耳朵。
他实际上不在听，
却意外听到了一种完全不同的听法——
那男孩发明了自己身上的聋，
他成了飞翔的、幻想的聋子。
　　　　会不会在凡人的落日后面
另有一个众声喧哗的神迹世界？
会不会另有一个人在听，另有一个落日
　　　　在沉落？
哦踉跄的天空
大地因没人接听的电话而异常安静。
机器和昆虫彼此没听见心跳，
植物也已连根拔起。
那小男孩的聋变成了梦境，秩序，乡音。
卡车开不动了
　　　　父亲在埋头修理。
而母亲怀抱落日睡了一会，只是一会，
不知天之将黑，不知老之将至。

Potato Brother (马铃薯兄弟)

Fruit Store in Twilight

The keeper of the fruit store, the lady
starts to scrub her oranges,
one by one
Her movements
gentle and beautiful,
as if to relive the long lost feel
of her hands

Her eyes rise above the oranges, those round and juicy oranges,
to somewhere far and hazy. Suddenly
something rolls from outside to inside her skin,
chilly or warm

She scrubs the oranges
one after another,
until the skin dries and shines
in the wrinkles of twilight,
serene and solitary

She puts the most radiant,
the most mellow orange
on top of all oranges
And then closes the store

Tomorrow, welcome
Tomorrow.

Translated by Sun Dong

水果店的黄昏

水果店的老板娘
又在擦拭她的橙子
她挨个擦拭
动作
温柔而优美
像在重温
失落已久的
手上的感觉

她眼神渺远
越过圆润的橙子
抵达远方
有什么忽然　在
皮肤的内外
滚动，沁凉或者温暖

她逐一擦拭
直到果皮干涩
在黄昏的褶皱里
发出安静　而
孤寂的光

她把最光洁
最圆润的
放在了最上面
然后
关上店门——

明天欢迎来买
我的橙子

Potato Brother (马铃薯兄弟)

The Fluid in the Twilight

The fluid in the twilight
enters my veins
through Spring and the syringe,
like the pretty but listless girl opposite me, we
share the same invasion
of dusk

She speaks, the girl from other places
so quiet and sweet
She brings a beverage and food for herself
and a tacky magazine, so
she is ready to scorn
the dark night

Night color enters her body
crawls to her pretty eyebrows
Her head settles on the wooden chair back

My arms feel cold too
easy sleep hits me
The girl opposite me breathes and speaks in somniloquy.

Translated by Sun Dong

黄昏的液体

黄昏的液体
沿着春天和注射器
正进入我的静脉
正如同
对面倦怠的漂亮女郎
我们的共同
在于接受着黑暗的入侵

异乡的女孩她开口说话
多么地安静，多么乖
她为自己准备了饮料和食品
还有一本俗气的杂志
她做好了蔑视黑夜的准备

夜色进入她的身体
漫上她漂亮的睫毛
她的头歪向了木质的椅背

我的手臂也感到了冷
随遇而安的睡意袭来
对面的女孩已发出轻轻的梦呓

Potato Brother (马铃薯兄弟)

Sad Looks in the City

A person
Walks along crying
all alone
Crying and walking
Nobody notices
Him or her
Maybe he or she has woe bigger than the sky
It doesn't get on the city's nerves
A person's sorrow
is like throwing a stone into the sea
I see a person's broken heart but I can't hear
his or her voice
flashes for a second and then
disappears.

Translated by Sun Dong

城市中的悲伤面孔

一个人
哭泣着走过
就是一个人
哭泣着走过
没有谁会留意
他或她
或许天大的悲伤
对于喧闹的城市和它的神经
一个人的悲伤
激不起任何动静
因此我看到
某个人只有悲伤的面孔
而没有声音
倏忽就闪过了

Potato Brother (马铃薯兄弟)

At the Tea House

Over mixed nuts
at the tea house, we
are like a bunch of bears
shelling and peeling

Something left over, a surplus—
the green leaves dive and
immersed in the transparent glass, stretch themselves
slowly, as if bathing in the sun
cooked and well done.

Translated by Sun Dong

在茶楼

来一盘坚果
在茶楼
我们像一群小熊
剥着果壳
多出来的
是绿色的叶子
装在透明的杯子里
慢慢舒展
仿佛在阳光下的样子
只是已经慢慢熟了

Potato Brother (马铃薯兄弟)

A Prison Guard in Love

It is morning, a prison guard in love
so gentle
Under the lime colored leaves
she lifts her face toward the sun
Happiness and the beauty of her femininity
irresistible
She is on the phone with her love, the sky is painted with
cherry blossoms

So she forgets the nightmares behind her
The walls before her too.

A prison guard walking on the streets,
Love makes her eyes lenient
delicate
Shining with human warmth.

Translated by Sun Dong

恋爱了的女狱警

早晨，一个恋爱的女狱警
多么温柔
一片嫩绿的树叶下
她的脸朝向阳光
喜悦和性别的美丽
毫无遮拦
她在和自己爱的人通话
天空开满了樱花

她因此而忘记了
后面的梦魇
前面的高墙

一个女狱警走在路上
爱情让她的眼神慈祥
纤弱
并发出人性的光芒

Potato Brother (马铃薯兄弟)

On a Crowded Morning Metro

Two girls are talking about carrying coffins
One with a blue scarf
One with a red scarf
The Red Scarf wears blue lipstick
The Blue Scarf wears red lipstick

They are talking about faraway places
about the Blue Scarf's brother
He is carrying coffins for a living
"Who isn't scared of it, but money is money,
you know"

In the morning, amid all that
the hustle and bustle,
People are about to plunge
into the business of
carrying coffins.

Translated by Sun Dong

早晨拥挤的地铁里

两个姑娘在谈论抬棺
一个围着蓝色的围巾
一个围着红色的围巾
红围巾配着蓝嘴唇
蓝围巾配着红嘴唇

她们在谈论远方
谈着蓝围巾的亲哥哥——
他在帮人抬棺
“谁不害怕啊，不过是为了钱而已”

在早晨，人们拥挤、奔波
即将开始投身于
那些类似抬棺人的事

Shen Qi (沈奇)

Thereafter

"Stop the world
I want to get off"

0
hazy moon
past lives born into this one

the Buddha said: settle in
Confucius said: travel far

1
see the world with open eyes
the Western wind and the dying sun
watchtowers of the house of Han

—thereafter
old nobility dissipates
poor children enjoy Western sounds

2
ever since the chrysanthemums withered
the poem's lines withered too—

sacred mountain
scrapped mountain

withered chrysanthemums
withered poetic tantrums

how haggard is he!

3
Confucius said: to miss a Classic
is to miss

尔 后

残句系列（节选）

Stop the world
I want to get off

——**题记**

0
月色朦胧
前世转而今生

佛说：入驻
子曰：旅行

1
睁眼看世界
正西风残照
汉家城阙

——尔后
老贵族风流云散
穷孩子喜欢洋调调

2
自从菊花开残
诗句也残了——
圣山
剩山

残菊
残句

斯人独憔悴！

3
子曰：错过古典
便是错过

黎明的呼吸

the breath of dawn
the Autumn winds lose their distant air
nobody treads the old paths

4
—thereafter
to the West
from the West

moving oceans and opening frontiers of
wet dreams
inoculations against "banana people"

5
—thereafter
empty trash
copy
paste
restart

copycat innovation
innovative copycats
taking another's land as one's motherland

6
—thereafter
the tempered rhymes of Chinese
got a style update

the *Book of Odes* for wet clothes
Song-lyrics for eulogies
Tang poems for candied *hu-lu* fruit
and……dancing in the public square

7
the hazed confusion of half past seven
a dog, a person, and a faraway place

the dog's gaze steadfast
the person's gaze dodgy

秋风失远意
故道少人行

4
——尔后
西来
西去

移洋开新的
梦遗
接种“香蕉人”

5
——尔后
清空
复制
粘贴
重启

模仿性创新
创新性模仿
却把他乡作故乡

6
——尔后
汉语的合辙押韵
换了新款式

诗经换了湿巾
宋词换了颂词
唐诗换了糖葫芦
以及……广场舞

7
……七点半的迷茫
狗，和人，和远方

狗的眼神实实在在
人的眼神虚虚晃晃
夕阳在楼群的后面

the sun sets behind a cluster of buildings
showing its face briefly, one sees

over in that faraway place
a girl wishing to enter the city

8
—thereafter
subtle, like the Way of Tea
drinking tea, becoming wind

subtle, like the Way of Poetry
writing poetry, becoming insane

and losing weight, or maybe
getting a bit more international

9
Confucius said: is it useful?

is drinking tea useful
is writing poetry useful
is going upstairs useful

if it's not useful
then how is it that so many
are drinking and writing
and fighting for a shot to go upstairs

if it is useful
then how is it that nothing has changed?!

10
even death has changed its tone
a uniquely modern death
a type of "mortgage"
where you "pay in installments"
inexorable anxiety that lasts all day long
a funeral with nowhere to bury one's heart

露了一下脸，看见

在那遥远的地方
有位想进城的姑娘

8
——尔后
茶道式微
喝茶成风

诗道式微
写诗成疯

以及减肥，或
与国际接轨

9
子曰：有用吗？

喝茶有用吗
写诗有用吗
上楼有用吗

如果没用
何以那么多人
在喝着在写着
在争先恐后上楼着

如果有用
何以什么也没有改变？！

10
连死亡也变调了
——现代性死亡
一种“按揭”
以及“分期付款”
惶惶不可终日
死无葬心之地

每一只眼睛后面

behind every eyeball
septwolves roam

11
—thereafter
little pig asks Mama pig
what's the meaning of living?

12
Confucius said: to speak
or not to speak
this is an issue

13
"we don't wash our hands often
but we wash our hearts daily"

a Tibetan painter
on the grasslands told me

when i returned to the city,
i washed my hands more diligently…

14
the dust is thick
as is the greyish mood of premodern times
it won't go away no matter how much you sweep

snowflakes are thin
as is the neo-Romanticism of postmodern times
it dissipates as soon as it hits the ground

15
Aaah, Mandarin in the morning—

holding hands
growing old together

picking chrysanthemums beneath the Eastern ivy
South Mountain breathes into view

跑着七匹狼

11
——尔后
小猪问猪妈妈
活着的意义是什么？

12
子曰：说
还是不说
这是个问题

13
“我们不常洗手
但天天洗心”

一位藏族画家
在草原上对我说

回到城里
洗手洗得更勤了……

14
灰尘很厚
前现代的灰心情也很厚
扫也扫不尽

雪花很薄
后现代的浪漫主义也很薄
落地就化了

15
古早味的汉语啊——

执子之手
与子偕老

采菊东篱下
悠然见南山
人语

stories of people
fables of things

early snow in the gentle wind
fragrance of plum blossoms slighting about

16
i've walked into submission and exhaustion
on this great road
no reason not to wind onto a smaller path
leisurely and carefree—

enter the dim willows and bright flowers
after washing your heart and clearing your eyes

you've become your own
"avant-garde"
or your own …… "lover"

17
Confucius said: in this world,
the greatest love
is: the one that within the object of affection
finds self-love—

a cup of wine amongst the flowers
we three, my shadow, the moon, and I

18
—thereafter
in the herpes blotches
of Modern Mandarin Chinese

you've understood Lu Xun
and Tao Yuanming

19
the Buddha said—

物语

初雪微风
暗香梅花消息……

16
大路走乏了
也走厌倦了
不妨弯到小路
优哉游哉—

柳暗花明中
洗心明目后

你成了你自己
的“先锋”
或……“情人”

17
子曰：这世上
最可珍重的爱
是：能从爱的对象中
爱到我自己——

花间一杯酒
对影成三人

18
——尔后
在现代汉语的
带状疱疹里

你理解了鲁迅
也理解了陶渊明

19
佛说——

to take a misunderstanding
and pursue it til the end
is enough to clearly see
the essence of “nothingness”

20
……when children
say “keep calm”
with an internet accent

all you can do
is stay behind with the old feelings
you have about “keeping calm”

21
—thereafter
Laozi asked the “new humans”

one begets two
two begets three
what does three beget?

answer: three begets utter rubbish!

22
—thereafter
Zhuangzi drummed on a basin

what is this eve, oh,
cellular telly, cellular telly
what, oh, is this eve,
bodhi, bodhi

love, ya-da-dee!

23
to lose and to return
text and flesh

将一种误会
坚持到底
就足以看清
“虚无”的本质

20
……当孩子们
以网络的口吻
说着“淡定”一词

你只能留守自己
“淡定”后面的
那一点旧心情

21
——尔后
老子问“新人类”

一生二
二生三
三生什么？

答曰：三生幺蛾子！

22
——尔后
庄子鼓盆

今夕何兮
手机手机
何兮今夕
菩提菩提

爱咋咋地！

23
失落与返回
文本与肉身

the vigor of a student
autumn feelings were borne of heaven

—in the deep crevasses of time
whose silhouette
turns upstream towards the dawn?

24
in days of yore, days before,
I walked amongst luxuriant grasses
—those remnants and pulses
of our ancestors

this eve I return, oh,
buildings towering high
—the clamor and exhaust
of the endless stream of cars

what is this eve, oh,
bodhi, bodhi

what, oh, is this eve,
cellular telly, cellular telly

25
Confucius said: water
always lives on the upstream flow

but those innocent sheep
have become accustomed
to obeying the wind's suggestions
gazing always and forever downstream…

26
at this juncture—
those who have been emptied by fate
will at the same time
empty "fate" itself

书生意气
秋意本天成

——时间的深处
谁的身影，转向
上游的黎明？

24
昔我往矣
芳草萋萋
——那祖先的
遗泽与脉息啊

今我归兮
高楼林立
——那车流的
轰鸣和尾气啊

今夕何兮
菩提菩提

何兮今夕
手机手机

25
子曰：水
总是在水流的上游活着

可那些无辜的羔羊
早已习惯了
顺从风的眼神
向下游张望……

26
当此关口——
被命运清空了的人
也便同时
清空了“命运”

—we can't go back
we can only disembark here!

27
—thereafter
the ostentatious return to ostentations,
the depressed return to depressions

how can one cast aside late years?
the clouds are so deep I can't tell where I am

28
—thereafter
The Revered One of the World picks flowers
Canaan smiles

29
—thereafter
hazy moon…

who was it on the riverbank that first saw the moon?
when was it the moon and river first bathed them in light?

written at Zhongnan Yinruo, late 2016

Author's note: the original composition is 82 verses and over 500 lines, and was published in Zhongshan literary bimonthly, 2017 vol. 2.

Translated by Benjamin Landauer

——我们回不去了
我们只能提前下车！

27
——尔后
浮华的归浮华
忧郁的归忧郁

何以掷迟暮
云深不知处

28
——尔后
世尊拈花
迦南微笑

29
——尔后
月色朦胧……

江畔何人初见月
江月何年初照人

2016 年岁末于终南印若居

原作82节500余行载《钟山》文学双月刊2017年第2期

Shu Yu (舒羽)

Osmanthus Flower Rain

If you come to Hangzhou
I will take you to get drenched in osmanthus rain
We will set out just after dawn
Make our way uphill on winding steps
At each turn you will see
Scented blossoms glistening with raindrops

In golden rain lit by the rising sun
Scattered blossoms will sift onto my hair
I'll say you have a youth's eyes, taking in all angles
Brimming with delicious kindness
You'll say that my laugh
Is like water scooped up in moonlight
Dancing in flecks that meet and part
While brewing a heady pot of osmanthus rain

Translated by Denis Mair

桂花雨

假如你来杭州
我会带你去淋一场桂花雨
我们将在清晨出发
沿着委婉的山道拾阶而上
你将看到那一湾一湾
满是明亮的芳华

当金色的光雨
一口一口吮着芬芳的呼吸
如雨的光明
一朵一朵筛落我黑色的发际
我说你的眼睛
是阳光下摇曳的少年
洋溢着喷香的热情
你说我的笑
是一掬摇碎的月光
一缕一缕，密密疏疏
酿醉了一壶桂花雨

Shu Yu (舒羽)

Cat

Again at the hour of midnight
Like a changeling born of an angel and a demon
A long breath followed by a pant, a yowl then a sigh
Such plaintive keening
Holding nothing back, a shrill and ragged whine
Innocent yet jaded, instinctive yet contrived
Mellow yet urgent, an exhalation followed by a gasp, or a note
of simmering resentment

Does such a cry come from being mired in lust
Or from deep in a female soul, made to languish alone in her bedroom?
Is it an angel's aria...or a demon's nightmare?
More terribly, it seems like a human voice that falls between all of these

It also seems like
A ceremony handed down since ancient times
That pair of emerald eyes in the darkness has the look
Of a priest making an offering to the dead
Or quickening living hearts
It comes from deep in the throat
More, it is driven by a force outside the body
It comes from within awareness
More, from outside of awareness
Where uncanny paradoxes are resolved
It is religion in sound
A performance but also a divination foretelling destiny
By a singer who specializes in spine-tingling melodies

At daybreak it hides away, like the lifting of mist
Not to get away from light, but to be with darkness

猫

又是午夜时分，
像天使与魔鬼产下的灵异的婴孩，
长一声，短一声，尖一声，叹一声——
如此哀伤凄厉、
恣意妄为、声嘶力竭的，
天真与世故、本能与矫作、
从容与紧迫、长吁与短叹的，甚至
充满着怨愤的声音。

是浸淫于欲望不能自拔的感官呼应？
还是空闺怨妇寂寞灵魂深处的呼喊？
是天使的咏叹，还是魔鬼的梦魇？
更可怕的，它仿佛是介于多者之间的
一种人类的声音。

又像是
一种古老但从未失传的仪式，
黑夜中，那一对绿石的眼睛
许是祭祀时必要的神情？
悼念死者的灵魂，
或召唤生者的意志？
它来自喉咙，
更来自身体之外的一种驱使；
来自意识，
更来自意识之外的
一种奇异的矛盾与统一。
它是声音的宗教，
是专事诡异之歌唱家的
一种直透命理的表演。

天一亮，就隐匿，如散去的雾。
不是因为光明，而是因为黑暗。

Yet it is only a cat
It is hard to connect those night sounds to what we see by day
Maybe this is why the cat is so mellow by day
So languorous and quiet
A cat has nine lives, and I believe it
But do not look straight into its eyes
It does not want to exchange glances with you
You are only a shape in outline, passing before its eyes

Translated by Denis Mair

但它只是猫。
人们无法将它与白天相联系。或许
这正是猫在白天之所以温顺娴静，
甚至慵懒的原因？
猫有九条命，我信。
但不要直视它的眼睛，
它并不想看你。
你只是它眼中的一条线状的
影子。

Shu Yu (舒羽)

Hearing Orioles in Willows and Waves

Just like a konghou[9] played with rapid and complex rhythm
Willows droop and segment the fog, thin or thick
With the swinging twelve-tone equal temperament
And performing with the shape of wind... with the creak of oar
Mountains and rivers become green, and here comes a gray rain
over West Lake. Therefore—

Every willow leaf is a final good-bye;
Every word is a star-voiced oriole.
The yellow oriole flying here brings back the message
Of the water running outside Qingbo Gate.
The yellow oriole flying there unfastens the watered silk of willows
Like dropping a button of mercury...

Cherishing the past and thinking of the present.
Old green willows have turned to snow with rain,
Swaying lightly in drizzle and unafraid in wild wind.
Who can decode the feminine features of the stories of time
By looking at the lines on her palm?

Who can play a grey and urgent harmonic curve
With the heart of a Konghou?
Juxtaposition and isomorphism. Though she has reproduced
South of the Yangtze River with the same curve,
It is just a part written by an idler with a virtual pen,
An event without intention while days
Are still green.

Listen! The oriole's wings wheeling and dripping...
Shuttling in the clear breeze, falling and rising in the green ripples,
And mending the silence of waves of light diligently.
Look! The track like an arrow in the air—
Penetrating the lake surface, the scalding setting sun,
And the place called "heart" by poets.

Translated by Bei Ta

---

[9] An ancient plucked stringed instrument

柳浪闻莺

宛如一架急管繁弦的箜篌，
柳儿倒垂，用十二平均律的摆荡
分割了雾霭的寡淡与浓稠，
演漾着风的形状……欸乃一声
绿了山水，西湖却下起了一阵
灰色的雨。于是——

每一片柳叶，都是一个诀别的词语；
每一个词语，都是一只流转的黄莺。
黄莺飞来，用星星的喉咙
带回清波门外流水的消息。
黄莺飞去，如脱落一枚水银的纽扣，
解开了杨柳带水的衣襟……

惜往与思今，依依复霏霏，
细雨中轻摇，狂风里不惧。
谁能自她披靡的掌纹中，
破译流年阴柔的情事？

谁又用箜篌的心，
弹奏一株灰白倥偬的倒影？
并置与同构。尽管她用同一种形象，
繁衍了一个千年的江南，
也只是散人笔下，那一个
虚笔带过的部分，
一个无心的事件。而日子
依然青郁。

听哪，黄莺轮翅，滴泠泠……
在清风里穿梭，绿浪间跌宕，
殷勤缝补着一片波光的寂静。
看哪，空中那一道如箭的轨迹——
穿过湖面，穿过滚烫的夕阳，
穿过那一个被诗人称为心的地方。

Shu Yu (舒羽)

Macao: Oficinas Navais

—To Yao Feng

Enclose the slaughterhouse of the past
and install blinds from the Contemporary Art Center.
Let the owner of the gambling house sit in the seat of honor
and listen to poets reading poems.
The light is perfect. There is a scent of Brazilian tobacco.
He holds his chin, his poinciana eye
ponders the limits of the Merchant of Venice.
He is surprised at those gamblers selling languages
and selling nihilist determination.
Whereas love is a shameful memory,
and sounds like a lie.
The proverbs in Macao are a piece of white marble stationery,
left in the cemetery, sandalwood fragrance drifting quietly.
The Portuguese freighters are glittering,
shuttling between Sunda Islands.
Lions are the only sailors,
scattering the dialects of pearls, spices, and fine porcelain.
Now they raise black veils, full of wind-blown tenderness,
sail from the Venetian's harbor, only to carry
a Persian daisy for a muse.

Translated by Chen Xing

澳门：海事工房

赠姚风

把昔日的屠场围起来，
再按上一幅当代艺术中心的百叶窗，
请赌场的老板坐首席，听诗人读诗。
光线正好。有巴西烟草的味道。
他托着下巴，用一只凤凰木的眼睛
拿捏威尼斯商人的分寸，
吃惊于这些兜售语言的赌徒
贩卖虚无的决心。
而爱是羞愧的记忆，
说出来犹如一句谎言。
亚妈港的箴言是一方汉白玉的信笺，
留在静静地飘着檀香的墓园。
葡萄牙人的货船呀金光闪闪，
穿梭于巽他群岛之间，
狮子是唯一的水手，
遍撒珍珠、香料与细瓷的方言。
而今升起黑色的帷幔，胀满风的柔情，
驶出威尼斯人的港湾，只为运载
一朵缪斯的波斯菊。

Shu Yu (舒羽)

Leave Before the Lights Go Out

This time,
I'll leave before the lights go out.
When the curtain rings down,
I'll leave the waves of applause
and the moving farewell speech
behind.

No one will care about the loneliness in a theater
when the play ends and the audience departs.
It will be a garden abandoned
after a passionate, armed visit from an emperor.
After the prosperity, who will care how the gardener
went from eagerness to despair?
No one will care about a faded actor,
his fervor after a tearful goodbye.
It will be a nightmare,
getting into costume and character
harder still to take off both.
After gongs and drums, who cares how an emperor
removes his crown and washes off life's vagaries?

There is no need to be sentimental, no need to cherish the illusion.
In an era chasing speed,
please keep the non-stop beat.
We are asked to build and destroy with the same meter.
Just leave, leave before the lights go out.
Don't get squeezed in the departing crowd.

Translated by Chen Xing

在灯光熄灭前离去

这一次
我在灯光熄灭前离去，
将落幕时那一浪浪掌声
和动人的告别陈辞
留在身后。

没有人会在乎一个剧场
曲终人散的冷寂，
那是一个帝王
热刺刺金戈铁马省亲后遗落的花园，
繁华过后，谁会在乎一个守园人的心，
如何从热切走向荒凉？
没有人会在乎一个倡优
含泪挥别后的炙热，
那是一个穿戏服入戏难，
脱戏服出戏更难的梦魇。
锣鼓声后，谁会在乎一位帝王
如何摘下王冠，洗出一脸沧桑？

何必感伤，何必缅怀那些虚妄。
在一个追求速度的时代，
请敲响马不停蹄的节拍，
我们被要求摧毁和建设同样的快。
走吧，在灯光熄灭前离去，
别拥在散场的人群里。

Shu Yu (舒羽)

Nights in the English Countryside

Nights in the English countryside were a nostalgic novel
written by a stranger with needle points and awns of wheat.
So many times, I was about to confess
how the flushing dark blueness outside the window
shook me blink by blink.
I wanted to tell you, that night, clouds were dipped with ink
bending down, capturing the moors;
I thought I saw Wuthering Heights.
I saw an obstinate girl sitting on the fence,
Her long hair covering her face.
Storms called for downpours.
The church was waiting for the bells of vespers.
Oh, the wind could not be seen. Only time
flapping its pale wings, glided across through atmosphere.
Tainted with too much landscape
It couldn't freeze-frame Van Gogh's strokes.
When the mist rose, the glass was stained with suspicion,
deepening the night with its layers, till the moon
turned biased with a withering thought
marked with Russian miseries.
So I thought, the fire would go out.
The body of a cello would mottle into a gravelly fate.
Whereas beauty was still a lonely scene,
like the nights in the English countryside, like unrepeatable love.
And my love—
was a tall palm frond with the slimmest body.
Only afraid of its being real, trembling,
in the wilderness in a strange land,
making a noise of something being hurt.

Translated by Chen Xing

英国乡村的夜晚

英国乡村是异乡人笔下
一部针尖麦芒上的乡愁小说。
很多次了，我差一点就要说出
窗外那一袭流溢的深蓝，
曾经怎样一遍遍地将我摇撼。
想告诉你那晚的云朵蘸饱了墨汁，
垂下身来，俘虏了麦田；
我仿佛看见了呼啸山庄，
看见一个倔强的女孩坐在篱笆上，
长发斜斜地，遮住了她的脸庞。
暴风呼唤骤雨，
教堂等待晚祷的钟声……
哦，看不见的是风，只有时间
扇动着灰白的翅膀在大气中滑翔，
它因为沾染了太多的风景，
而无法定格成凡•高的笔触。
雾霭升起的时候，玻璃充满了怀疑，
一层一层加深了夜晚，直到把月亮
偏颇成一枚凋敝的思念，
带着俄罗斯式的苦难。
于是我想，炉火会熄灭，
大提琴的身体会斑驳成嘶哑的命运，
而美，依旧是一幕孤独的剧情，
像英国乡村的夜晚，像不可复述的爱情，
而我的爱情——
是一棵高高的棕榈叶，有着最细碎的身体，
怕只怕弦儿动了真情，颤栗着，
在异乡的旷野，发出了
被什么弄痛了似的声音。

Sun Dong (孙冬)

Mid-autumn at Kamakura

On Mid-autumn Day
Arrows fall like tornadoes
The silence summoned for reinforcement
rests on the tatami of
the Zen temple.

Translated by Sun Dong

中秋在日本镰仓

在中秋
弓矢如瀑流

受命于危难之时的寂静
落在禅院的
榻榻米上。

Sun Dong (孙冬)

Fire

Healed from amnesia, the fire
returns silently after many years

The old house reaches out to it instantly
Its eggs hatched before even touching its body

The dusk encloses from four frontiers yet
Sparsely scattered from each other
Every single spark
Is drifting from its soul

Fire must have wanted to know in great depth
the extreme form of nostalgia
The pain of the field aspiring and keeping itself open
Is vehemently consoled in
fire

We call fire a wounded healer
At the burnt wrist of grass
fire licks itself
The world is pulled to stop for just one
minute

A silky path revealing itself
on the paper.

Translated by Sun Dong

火

多年之后，失忆的火
悄然回归

老房子伸出自己
游动的卵来不及接触感伤
就崩出干柴

暮霭四合而疏略
每一粒灰烬
都灵魂出鞘

火一定是想深刻了解
乡愁的极端形态
田野因广阔而饱受的痛苦
在剧烈地得到安慰

我们叫他带伤的治愈者
在野草腰黑处
火舔了一下自己
世界仿佛安静了片刻
仿佛一段
柔顺丝滑的道路
跃然纸上。

Sun Dong (孙冬)

Libertine, Night Guard and Roamer

Real shops are scarcer and scarcer
More like specimens of the obsolete capital
A libertine does not have anything to see
He even doesn't have the change
to give to the beggars

A Roamer is in the cloud
He never rests, the auxiliary police removes the
hinge, giving the traffic a push to reach its maximum capacity

At Down Square, we exchange things that jolted us
into anger and then into silence, the night guard pumped,
and fluttered at our presence

Endless roaming consumes the libertines excited the
night guards possessed
our names

None of the corners are turning points
No parallels on the other side
Those at large can't escape without navigation systems
Even the storm in the smart toilet
is programmed at precise times

Get ready, scavengers in the human manuscripts,
To welcome the sun in your past,
The wasteland will wash up and head to pillow
The sun also rises
tomorrow.

Translated by Sun Dong

浪荡子守夜人和漫游者

街边的店面越来越少
像是几个旧资本时代的标本
一个浪荡子没什么可看
他身上甚至没有小钱
连乞丐也不知所终

一个漫游者在云里
他从不歇息，协警将悬日提速
助其抵达

在曙光广场，
我们聊着一天的突发事件
无感，气泵上的守夜人
被莫名鼓舞

是无尽的浪荡掏空了你
是守夜兴奋了他
还是我们被漫游者盗取了身份

每一个拐角都不是节点
怎么办，
那些携信号潜逃者在
导航里搁浅
连智能马桶的风暴
也控制在精确的时间

还在大量人类生活脚本里
拾荒的浪荡子你们在过去里
进入曙光吧
荒原要洗洗睡了
明天太阳照常上班。

Sun Dong (孙冬)

A Letter to Smog

This city has a middle name
Mrs. Birdless' motel
A girl smokes in smog
Talent might dissipate after a while
At this wandering hour
You are still reluctant to exchange your white lie
for my treasure

Translated by Sun Dong

给雾霾写一首诗

这个城市又名
百鸟不宿
雾霾里
一个女孩在抽烟，很多方案在
生效，才华苦捱一会儿就会消散，
在游荡的午夜
他仍不肯拿无聊之物和我的
宝贝交换。

Sun Dong (孙冬)

The Red Moon

The faint murmur from the inside
of the craft overwhelms the
jeering of NASA

I follow the vehicles to the orgy, consuming, forgetting
and excusing my little brain

My proxy is not far
Poor signal and
I am not sure it is waiting for me
I see too many blind attractions, too many
rotten targets

My body looks elsewhere, its hood is throwing
bad breath to outer-space, meet my host and all her

hostages, meet the primitive
night every million years and jointly we
float to where the crash happened

A Red Moon rises up in arms, no wonder
the traffic moves at turtle speed
Our black box is full of rain checks of a country
meant to build the red power under
the historical shadow of the
Sun

Tonight the heavenly dog passes by
Everybody is endorsing its project
Until my presence is his and the sky
burns above the Moon Bay Boulevard
not far from
my vehicle, my
Universe.

Translated by Sun Dong

红月亮

机器深处发出的微弱杂音
甚至压倒
国家宇航局的浪笑
我在晚归的路上随着
车河游荡
进入正在被自己遗忘的狂欢
家在不远处
它的信号微弱
隔着盲目的吸引力
我不确定它在等我
它更像是看向别处的风景
那些焦急地翻阅房间的油烟
也飘向窗外
连这城市的夜晚也
被百年一遇的人们挟裹着
走向失事的方向
一枚红月亮反了，难怪
前方星星通行缓慢
那轮布满血丝的黑匣子
藏着国家的雨支票
在太阳的历史背影下正在形成
阴谋得逞的红色势力
今晚有天狗出没
就是这个机器
在背书，我还在悬挂物的阴影之下
随着车河游荡
咫尺之外
月亮湾大道上已经
燃烧了起来。

Sun Dong (孙冬)

Wall

Geologic change is too slow
a species goes extinct too slowly the years roll on
everything is the opposite of poetic
the carrot top was a little conspirator Brodsky also drank gutter oil
that guard Micaiah can only say drily
you can cough when you're at home
crime usually occurs in the train station of the heavenly realm or in
Notre Dame de Paris who can expect
a black rider darker than the black horse towering
outside the wall outside the foam of thick language
probing
some corner of the wall
excavating the interpreters they say
speaking without reserve means you can speak forever
minding your own business is a virtue
looking, listening, asking, feeling are methodology after that
digging out the earthworms cockroaches and flies they say
making the whole world harmonious is dirty work
fastidious people always have some unfastidious aspects
and in the end, what gets dug out are ordinary bones
although you are outstanding men and women or
beautiful barbels and big-eyed shelducks none of it is worth a penny
in fact there is only one powerful thing
the symptoms of sclerosis
it would shake things up too much if everybody and his dog became immortal
who can hear the sound of the chamber bursting and of whispering and burning
and fright
outside the world's bandwidth

Translated by Josh Stenberg

墙

一种地理变化太慢
一种动物灭绝太慢 年华衮衮
一切均和诗意相反
胡萝卜头是个小阴谋家 布罗茨基也喝过泔水油
米该雅这个守望者 也只能干巴巴地说
在你的家里可以咳嗽
罪行发生通常在 天国火车站 或是
巴黎圣母院 有谁期待
比黑马更黑的骑手 兀立于
迷墙之外， 于匝实的语言泡沫之外
探入
一段墙角
挖出解读者 他们说
言无不尽是说可以永远说下去
独善其身是一种是善
望闻问切是一种方法论 随后
挖出蚯蚓蟑螂和苍蝇 他们说
天下大同是一个脏活
讲究人总有不讲究的地方
最后挖出的是普通的尸骨
任凭你是出色的男人和女人 或是
漂亮的鲍鱼和大眼睛的麻鸭 都最不值钱
强大其实只是一个
硬化症症状
羽化成仙或者鸡犬升天的动静太大
有谁听到腔室爆裂和耳语和燃烧和恐惧的声音
在世界的波段之外......

Sun Dong (孙冬)

Rain Shelters Us in the City

We tremble
Two loose screws talking in rain's language

blend into inseparable mandate, rain, us and our distorted apartments
shelter my demon like secret does intervene
the television tower and turn their
pied lights off, pouring cats and gods
let them lick each other's tails

So good this nagging voice of loneliness, or whatever this city grows
in me got bleached in the rain, I can't stand the Alipay[10]
the perjury of family dinner or the translucent clouds which store
my moments

The rain restores our classical fear
a hundred bags of broken words are collected
In this southern city of
Nanjing.

Original written in English by Sun Dong

---

[10] Alipay is a service in China similar to PayPal

(Original written in English)

Tian Yuan (田原)

Half of Hong Kong

Half reclines on mountains, cars cruising steep, twisted roads,
Half surrounded by ocean, ships drifting on ocean.

Half the tall buildings vie for blue sky,
Half the cramped houses worry in shadows.

Half the passengers snoozing on city buses,
Half the Cantonese on the subway shouted in a fever pitch.

Half luxury, half cheap,
Half smiles, half irritation.

Half the greasy rich people live in vacation homes,
Half the poor wear ragged clothes to sleep in rabbit hutches.

Half the temples choke with lingering incense,
Half the churches cleanse the heart with bells.

Half autocracy, half democracy,
Half homeland, half foreign.

Half the yearning filled with despair,
Half the despair filled with yearning.

Half the Indians left their Bodhisattva in oblivion,
Half the Filipina maids left their children back home to play the role of mother.

Half its people are born and bred,
Half its people immigrants or exiles.

Half its mother tongue bitterly homesick,
Half its accent heavy with the scent of butter.

Half its history dons western fashion,
Half its future cannot be guaranteed.

半的香港

一半靠山，车在盘山道上跑
一半环海，船在海面上漂

一半的高楼争夺蓝天
一半的陋居背阴里懊恼

一半的乘客公交车上打盹
一半的粤语地铁上高谈阔论

一半的豪华一半的廉价
一半的微笑一半的焦躁

一半的富人油头肥耳住着别墅
一半的穷人衣衫褴褛睡在鸽笼

一半的寺庙，缭绕的香火呛人
一半的教堂，悠扬的钟声洗心

一半独裁一半民主
一半故国一半异乡

一半的向往里充满绝望
一半的绝望里充满向往

一半的印度人忘却菩萨
一半的菲佣撇下儿女扮演母亲

一半的人土生土长
一半的人迁徙流亡

一半的母语有苦涩的乡愁
一半的方言里夹杂着洋腔

一半的历史洋装在身
一半的未来难以确认

Tian Yuan (田原)

Half the signs faded traditional characters,
Half the doorplates English taking root.

Translated by Jordan A. Y. Smith

一半招牌上的繁体字漂泊
一半门牌上的英文扎根

Tian Yuan (田原)

Shanghai

1
The harbor concerned with water levels,
Dividing the ocean with a single embankment,
Amidst the familiar sound of lapping waves
Fluffs up the pillow and sleeps.

2
Muddied river water
Bears tidings from Three Gorges,
Flowing into the inlet, this moment
Of clarity.

3
Towers crowding, jostling in the sky,
Hiding at times, appearing at times,
Streets surge with a tireless pedestrian wave
Roaming in unknown directions.

4
The Settlement is a scar in history,
Pain rendered vogue,
Birthmarks on mother tongues of the Red Gang, the Green Gang,
But vanishing memories.

5
The architectural range stands proud,
Oblivious to sinking foundations;
Nest construction occasions
Birds to fret.

6
Shanghainese, spoken in the Wu dialect,
Long ago was a unicorn,
More comedy than a one-man-show,
Shutting out the standard tongue.

上海

1
码头提防着水位
与大海一堤之隔
在听惯的涛声里
高枕无忧

2
浑浊的江水
带来峡谷的问候
在入海口的一刹那
变清

3
拥挤的空中楼阁
时隐时现
街道上人流涌动
迷失方向

4
租界是一块历史疤痕
痛疼成为时尚
洪帮青帮是母语的胎记
已被遗忘

5
楼群耸立
无视地面的下沉
鸟儿们为筑巢
伤透了脑筋

6
吴音里的上海话
是古老的独角兽
比独角戏滑稽
把普通话排斥在外

7
Ships leave docks
Sent off by seagulls,
Sails torn by ocean winds
Salute shipwrecked sailors.

8
Whether lice got into Eileen Chang's underclothes—
No one knows.
Whoever concocted sordid rumors about Soong Meiling
Has vanished from this world.

9
At four meters above sea level,
The eternally unwithering white magnolia
Strives to bloom between a junk and a propeller,
Not a single flower blooms without the embrace of that scent.

10
The Bund converts teardrops into jewels
Windows in the City God Temple reflect antiquity,
Bracelets in the Tianzi Fang glitter in jazz rhythms,
No telling the genuine from the counterfeit.

11
The West in the East
The East in the West
Business suits and China dress
Well-tailored to reality and ideal alike.

12
At the continent's eastern shore,
Nestled up to the ocean,
Bidding farewell to the distant sunset,
Bidding welcome to the nearby sunrise.

Translated by Jordan A. Y. Smith

7
驶出船坞的船
去迎接海鸥
海风吹破的帆
呼唤遇难的水手

8
没人知道
张爱玲的内衣是否寄生过虱子
跟宋美龄风流过的人
早已离世

9
海拔四米高的陆地上
长开不败的白玉兰
争艳在沙船和螺旋桨之间
它的馨香力压群芳

10
外滩让眼泪变成宝石
城隍庙的窗棂映现从前
田子街的手镯在爵士乐里泛光
真假难辨

11
东方里的西方
西方里的东方
西装与旗袍
跟现实和理想最相配

12
在陆地的东端
与大海厮守
远距离目送夕阳
近距离迎来日出

Tian Yuan (田原)

The Novelist
—for Yan Lianke

1
A single rope connected to your hometown,
No matter how much you travel, how far you go,
It pulls on your soul
With an invisible power.

2
The low straw roof
To highlight the tiny garden,
Seeds of the aged elm
To sate the hunger.

3
The muddy narrow road to the entrance
records your growth,
The remote town's
Only longing.

4
At the edge of town, rice paddies have dried up.
Finally, meaning is revealed,
All the eggs taken from the bird nests,
The trees unbearably lonely.

5
Over the mountain's divide,
You pull your one-ton wagon,
The carved furrows,
Scars in earth.

6
Sounds of the insects' chorus
Wrapped in fabled, distant thunder,
The nocturnal darkness provides
One more theater for bats in flight.

小说家
——给阎连科

1
故乡是一根拴魂的绳
游子走多远
它都会无形地
牵着你

2
低矮草房衬托
逼仄的院落
老榆树上的榆钱
充填饥饿

3
门前泥泞的小路
记载着你的成长
远方的城镇
是唯一的向往

4
村头的田湖干涸了
方呈现出意义
鸟巢里的蛋被掏光了
树才感到孤寂

5
山是一种阻挡
你拽着一吨的板车
刻下的辙印
是大地的伤痕

6
在虫鸣的合唱里
由远而近的闷雷带有寓言性
在蝙蝠的飞翔里
黑夜是另一类舞台

7
The dry crumbling sounds of withered wild mugwort
Enticing you to sprinkle it into the stove,
The burnt wildflowers a medicine patch
Plastered onto the rice fields in your hometown.

8
You are a ship sailing
Across the divide between reality and fiction,
You are a piece of charcoal burning
Yourself to ash, yet cannot stave off the bitter cold.

9
The dog who fed on the food you chewed for him died of old age.
You buried him under the tree in the park where you always took walks,
So that the dog's pale spirit
Would be able to find its way home.

10
The novelist is a great big tree,
A structure in the trunk where the woodpecker lodges.
Verbal leaves fan out to cut off sunlight, moonlight, starlight
Narrative fruits pelted with hail, sending nonsense scattering.

11
Piled up pages of manuscripts are plowed rice paddies,
The embankment roads between them, a grid linked to the universe.
The mother tongue is an absolute.
What crosses through
Is literature, the wings of its reality and magic.

12
The bugle of the morning sun summons up the paralyzed ideals.
Wish we could turn gunstocks into fence posts
To tether peace to them.
Wish we could turn battle flags into gauze
To wrap the bleeding sunset.

7
枯萎的野艾蒿窸窣作响
哀求着被填进炉灶
烧过荒的田
像一块贴在家乡的膏药

8
你是一艘船
摆渡在现实与虚构之间
你是一块炭
燃尽自己，却驱不走严寒

9
吃你嚼碎食物的小白狗老死了
把它埋在散步的花园树下
让小狗的魂记住
回家的路

10
小说家是一棵大树
结构的枝干里住着啄木鸟
语言的叶子剪碎阳光、月光和星光
情节的果实被冰雹击中，荒诞陨落

11
一摞摞稿纸是一块块耕田
阡陌纵横与宇宙相连
母语是绝对的
超越它，取决于
文学那双现实与魔幻的翅膀

12
晨曦的号角唤醒麻木的理想
你想让枪托变成木桩
拴住和平
你想让军旗变成纱布
包扎失血的残阳

13
For a sin under the sunlight,
Good sense is but a sigh.
In that grave atop the earth
Whose life is restored?

14
For us, the living dead,
The scales of time measure
Not our flesh
But the weight of our words.

Translated by Jordan A. Y. Smith

13
面对阳光下的罪恶
良知仅仅是一声感叹
面对大地上的墓冢
谁的生命能够复原？

14
我们都是活着的死者
时间的天平称量的
不是肉体
而是文字的重量

Tian Yuan (田原)

SMALL TOWN

Heading south, along memories reined in
By a story, in a little waterfront town
A barking dog from another era
Stirs the sadness of a sojourning heart
A pillaged farmhouse is restored by words
Deep in a crystalline pond
Stars of that era are still seen on fish scales
Gleaming under water

Across such a gulf of years
The river is a weary bandage
Enwrapping the wounded village and hills
A dock that has witnessed ordeals
Affords a view of rippling reflections
As if awaiting an emaciated boatman
With a sporadic cough
Who will return against the current
Rowing a boat with rattan canopy

In an old, straight tree
A few sparrows are chirping
Counting footfalls on flagstones
Inside a dilapidated temple
A monk reaching quietude
Enters heaven in a dream

The boatman's song is heard faintly
Resounding downstream
But water that bears his boat
Cannot carry away coughing sounds
Mingled with the piping of heaven

The clear sky is a mirror
Showing blemishes of memory
Inverted reflections of an era
Waver on the water's surface
And lose their clarity

小镇

循着叙述垄断的记忆
南下，在临水的小镇上
一声邂逅的狗叫
唤起我的羁愁

毁于兵燹的木楼被文字还原
清澈的水里
鱼鳞带着那时的星光
在水底闪亮

隔着那么长的岁月
河流是一条疲惫的绷带
它包扎着受伤的村落和山岗
沧桑的码头
翘望一片粼粼之水
仿佛在等待消瘦的水手
伴随着一阵阵咳嗽
划着乌篷船
逆流而归

挺拔的老树上
叽叽喳喳的麻雀
数着青石路上的跫音
残破的古庙里
圆寂的和尚梦见天堂

隐隐约约传来的船歌
回荡在下游
载动船的水
却流不走
那夹杂在天籁里的咳嗽

无遮无拦的天
是一面镜子
反照出记忆的黑斑
一个时代的倒影
在水中晃动
变得模糊不清

Tian Yuan (田原)

At a little town along the way
Strangeness is less strange when wrapped in darkness
In a dream I cough up blood
Then see the old boatman
The rhythmic glow of his pipe
Lights up my face

Translated by Denis Mair

旅次小镇
在陌生感被黑暗冲淡的夜晚
我在梦中咳血
然后梦见
老水手那明明灭灭的烟袋锅
照亮我的脸

Tian Yuan (田原)

DEATH OF A BUTTERFLY

In glorious autumn sunshine
My busy steps were brought up short
By a butterfly I nearly crushed underfoot
At first I thought she was resting by the road
I bent down for a look
Only to find her breath had ceased

She must have died only moments before
Her two antennae still wavered in the wind
Her fine legs still had strength to grip the ground
Sunlight shone through her darkened eyes
Her spotted wings refracted forlorn hues
Her beauty lay in a serenity
More complete than when she lived

Her death made me think of beautiful words
But no beautiful words could describe her death
Without thinking I took her in my fingers
And put her on the lawn, where people aren't allowed
This burial was most fitting for her

I will never forget that patch of grass
On the east-west street before the Station
At the first crossing, beneath a power line.

Translated by Denis Mair

蝴蝶之死

一个阳光明媚的晚秋
突然让我在午后收拢住匆匆脚步的
是路边差一点被我一脚踩在脚下的蝴蝶
起初，我以为她是在歇息翅膀
等我蹲下细瞧
才知道她已绝了呼吸

她一定是刚死不久
头上的两根长须还在随风轻摇
细长的腿还保留有抓紧大地的力量
阳光穿透她戴着墨镜的眼
斑斓的翅膀折射出凄凉的死亡之光
死去的蝴蝶是美丽的
她的美丽在于
死了比活着还显得安祥

她的死让我想起许多美丽的词句
但什么样的词句都无法描绘出她的死亡
我下意识地
用手指把蝴蝶小心地捏起
放进禁止入内的人工草坪上
这可能是对她最好的埋葬

那块草坪我永远不会淡忘
在站前东西大马路的第一个十字路口
一根高压电杆旁

Un Sio San (袁紹珊)

Nude Picnic

Such a dazzling autumn day, the trees in shabby garments
Someone's gaze is frozen so he perspires grossly
Only light can prance as freely as a horse

Little sister strolls in the water, I bathe on the shore
Someone extends his arm, a snake's protruding tongue
The straw mat covered in spilled apples and virtue

Porno ink fixes stacked legs as gymnastics or dance
And autumn leaves spread wide the forgiving wilderness
Providing cover for a thousand suspicious leopards.

Countless keys slide into lubricated keyholes
How many times have men's eyes, bourgeois genteel,
Relieved little sister and me of our coats?

Sister is always a rain-slick snail, glistening throughout with fragile light
While I, before her prince, brandish a cactus, a length of silk,
Haggling over the rate and number of his infidelities

But in this bright countryside, my body is her chamber
And the balloon of thought grows ever vaster
Absorbing ever more oxygen, desire, torment, hatred

Oh sister, in this whole universe
No living things are talked about more than we
And here amidst nature, I the poet have taken pains to be concise.

Translated by Jeremy Tiang

裸體野餐

在這樣明媚的秋天，樹木衣衫襤褸
有人因凝視而大汗淋漓
唯有光，可以放縱如一匹馬兒

妹妹在水中散步，我在陸上沐浴
有人伸出手，像一條蛇伸出舌頭
草蓆盡是翻倒的蘋果和良知

色情的油墨，把交疊的腿定義為體操或歌舞片
秋葉擴充著野地的寬容
又藏著一千隻可疑的豹了

無數鑰匙伸進油潤的鎖孔
紳士們的眼睛多少次，以資產階級的禮儀
為我和妹妹拿下了大衣

妹妹始終是雨後的蝸牛，渾身灑滿脆弱的光點
我在她的王子面前，拿出仙人掌與綢緞
討價還價他外遇的機率

但在這樣明媚的野地，她的房間就是我的身體
思想的氣球膨脹著
吸引更巨大的氧氣、欲望、疼痛、敵意

啊，妹妹，在宇宙之中
我們已成為被議論最多的生物
在野地之中，我身為詩人已盡力使事物簡潔

Un Sio San (袁紹珊)

DOGTRACK

I won't ask foolish questions, such as
Why must the dog run?
It could refuse to run.

I also won't ask, for instance,
Why pursue a mechanical bunny?
It could refuse to go faster.

The song of progress blares out loud
It is the work of machines to wear the animals down.
I, too, ran on that track, sunning away my childhood,
Now the grind of work pummels and pulls me apart.

The gate flies opens, and someone
Keeps striking the starting gong, a beehive. Women sit wearing hats, even at night,
I sit too, ten fingers tapping my keyboard
A greyhound in its sandpit, four legs pounding around its cycle, its hell.

As if those on the field were just waiting for the show to end,
As if they curve into a question mark and that were the answer,
As if the world were only black and white,
Divided into owners and workers, gamblers and gawkers.

In their World of Difference, they perform their noisy pantomime.
As for us, these loyal friends,
When we require a response, they lift a leg.

Translated by Jeremy Tiang

賽狗場

我不會問這種傻問題，比如，
狗為什麼要跑？
牠可以拒絕奔跑。

我也不會問，比如，
為什麼要追逐一隻電動小白兔？
牠可以拒絕速度。

進步主義的歌在奏鳴，
機器的工作是損耗牠們；
我也曾在那跑道曬黑了童年，
如今被單調的工作反覆按摩、撕裂。

閘口已開，有人
不斷把起步鐘敲成蜂窩。女人們在黑夜也戴帽坐着
我也坐着，用十指敲打鍵盤，
格力狗在沙圈，用四肢跑輸了牠的輪迴、地獄。

彷彿上場的只等待完場，
彷彿牠們躬成一個問號就是答案，
彷彿世界非黑即白，
分坐成主人工人、賭徒看客。

與別不同的牠們繼續演着喧鬧的默劇，
對於我們這種忠誠朋友，
必要時會撒一泡尿來回答。

Un Sio San (袁紹珊)

AMERICAN DREAM

I've never been to New Jersey
But recline in an Asian bed with my Chinese dream
While my dream self sneaks away
To New Jersey smoking plastic opium

A heartfelt call to say she arrived safely
My credit cards shredded with use
She sends postcards too
Bank statements red with lipstick kisses

The bank clerk says New Jersey me
Was quite the big spender as I slept
All the usual things:
Food drugs condoms vitamins
Maybe she has a kid to raise
I let her off the hook
It can't be easy living in a powerful country

My American dream shattered long ago
Leaving tie-dye shreds and *Jersey Boys: The Musical*
Sometimes I dream my country's strong as a python
Sometimes this comes true
In my dreams I'm thoroughly bad
Why won't the world's policeman teach me a lesson?

I've never been to New Jersey
I hear everyone there's a tough guy
Even their poetry
Is heavy metal and rap

Many people at my doorstep
Have no American dream
Or Chinese dream
New Jersey me never dreams I dream of her

I hear dreams are the flip side of real life
And only tough guys don't dream
Only I, who have never been to New Jersey, long for it
Only I, fragile in spirit, dream of strong countries

Translated by Jeremy Tiang

美國夢

還沒去過新澤西州
一直在亞洲的床上做著中國夢
我的分身從夢中不辭而別
逃到我還沒去過的新澤西州抽塑膠鴉片

深刻地報了平安
她把我的信用卡刷爆了
寄來明信片
紅紅的月結單充滿唇印

銀行職員說那個新澤西州的我
在我睡覺的時候到三間藥房裝大款
消費模式倒是雷同
不外乎食物、藥妝、避孕套和維他命丸
說不定家裡還有小孩要養
就饒了那個我吧
活在強國也挺不容易

我的美國夢早就碎了
只剩下嬉皮紮染頭巾和澤西男孩音樂劇
有時夢到自己的國家壯得像蟒蛇般嚇人
有時如願以償
夢裡成為徹頭徹尾的壞人
世界警察怎麼還不來教訓我呢

還沒有去過新澤西州
聽說那裡的人都是狠角色
連唸詩
都要重金屬和饒舌

我的家門口也有許多人
沒有美國夢
也沒有中國夢
新澤西州的那個我大概也不會夢到我夢到她吧

聽說夢是現實的反面
聽說無夢的人都是狠角色
只有我這個沒去過新澤西州的人朝思暮想
只有我這個做強國夢的心靈脆弱

MRS. ROBINSON AT THE HOTEL ESTORIL

His body
Was born in a barn
His virginity
Vanished with the summer

Becoming an octopus, a peacock
While his heart turned holy
Setting down its complex baggage
To embark on
The slow
Sermon of the world

A cocktail of enlightened spirits and sweat
The choppy world has no buoys
No lifeguards, no lanes
His nakedness is naked
His laziness is lazy
Soaking in youth, he gets drunk on it
His erections have erections
Eighteen feet across
Forty-four high
"Hormone floods ahead, mind your step"
Seduction is globalism *a la mode*

Bruised flowers bloom at the foot of the wall
Don't kiss too quickly, that's a poem without line breaks
Rubbing new pistils together
And perhaps again in twenty years
The dampened soul dries in the shade
He's thought of ending it
And leaving this place
Giving up on the dawn
Salmon fighting the current till death

Many years later he brings his daughter
To Piscina Municipal for laps
Soaking in time he sees fallen Estoril
Remembers how, by new-glazed windows

愛都的羅賓遜太太

他的肉身
在馬廄中誕生
他的童貞
跟著夏天消失

化作章魚或孔雀
而他心為聖徒
卸下繁文縟節的包袱
開始
世界
漫無章法的傳道

啟蒙的烈酒和汗水互相勾兌
深淺不一的世界沒有浮標
沒有救生員也沒有動線
他赤裸了他的赤裸
慵懶了他的慵懶
泡在青春成為徹底的酒鬼
勃起之後還是勃起
橫5.7米
高13.6米
「前方荷爾蒙土石流請注意」
引誘是盛行的國際主義

瘀青的花朵開在牆角
吻別來得太快了詩都來不及分行
只能互相抹上新的批盪
說不定二十年後可以重新在一起
讓滴水的靈魂在陰影中晾乾
他也曾想過一了百了
從此繞道不見
不再期盼晨曦
像逆流產卵的鮭魚力竭而死

多年後他帶著女兒
到新花園泳池鍛煉
泡在歲月中看破落的愛都
想起曾在每個嶄新的玻璃窗前

He made vivid, short-lived love
Stepping steadily
Across
Adulthood's cruel threshold
Watching Jacob wrestle the angel
Growing practiced, the tiger returns to the mountain,
The sun and moon playing witness

He once lived bright as a brass band
But now he plays pianissimo
For memory, a mosaic
Mrs. Robinson superimposed on every naked woman
Also whales, satin ribbons, birds, ship masts
Wine glasses, foliage
The shameful
Sickle
He longs to be wrapped in happiness
Ignoring the holes in the plot
Desirous of prime numbers, divisible only by one and themselves

Soaking in silence, watching fallen Estoril
Stillness becomes a good thing
Witnessing time the thief stealing treasures
The crane of death stands ready
So new people can replace the old
New buildings revitalize old districts
Gratifying the so-called majority who loved disappearances
Laying foundations
Taming
The dangerous
The permanently changed
Fengshui's fatal lack of foresight

Mrs. Robinson, dear Mrs. Robinson
He's still seventeen, still in you-topia
Frantically plucking raspberries
And tulips
Passing the square I see curvy women, identical builds
I eloped with him so I must try to be different from you

製造短命的愛栩栩如生
穩步
進入
殘酷的成人門檻
看雅各與天使摔跤
技藝漸趨純熟，以至放虎歸山，日月為鑑……

曾經活得過份響亮，像銅管樂
為此他加上弱音器
為回憶打上馬賽克
每個裸女疊加上羅賓遜太太
疊加上鯨魚、緞帶、飛鳥、船桅
酒杯、樹葉
和羞恥的
鐮刀
他渴求快樂的圍堵
像忽略情節中最大的漏洞
只求化成1和自身外無法被其他自然數整除的質數

泡在沉默中看破落的愛都
靜止變成一件美好的事
如同目擊歲月的歹徒劫走一批珍寶
死亡的起重機準備就緒
讓新人取代舊人
讓新樓重整舊區
設下
馴服的
危險的
無法還原的
致命又短視的風水
答謝熱愛消逝的所謂大多數

愛都的羅賓遜太太親愛的羅賓遜太太
他還留在十七歲他還活在異托邦裡
拼命採摘覆盆子
和鬱金香
路過廣場我看到每個渾圓裸女構造相同
我跟著他私奔了我只能努力活得和你不相像

Passing by Estoril, its profane invitation, I see
I see the desperation of loving a city
I see that to live
Is to draw endlessly from indecision
I see him look at me
The way he looks at
Thousands of naked women, strangers
Forever dipping bamboo baskets in the river of love
And coming up empty

Translated by Jeremy Tiang

路過愛都就能看到褻瀆的邀請
看到愛一座城市的無能為力
看到活著
就是對徬徨的無盡汲取
看到他看著我
就像
看著千百個過路的陌生裸女
在愛河中永恆地竹籃打水

Wang Jiaxin (王家新)

October Poem

When other poets in another world
sing bronze poems of October,
I walk into the only park on our street.
It's tiny, no bird walkers or Tai Chi exercisers, no one
except eucalyptus breathing hard in the haze.
Despondent roses like shamed brides
ginkgo leaves on the lawn, dead butterflies.
No hint of wind, only sweating stones
huddled together, a shrub of wild peach
is still in its dream.
All seems to be in order—
and the repetitious sound of desperate trimming
replaces the birds chirping.

Translated by Joan Xie

十月之诗

当另一些诗人在另一个世界
歌咏着十月的青铜之诗，
我走进我们街头唯一的小公园；
没有遛鸟的人，没有打太极的人，没有任何人，
只有楞树在雾霾天里艰难呼吸；
玫瑰垂头丧气，让我想起蒙羞的新娘，
飘落在草地上的银杏树叶子，
则像一些死去的、不再挣扎的蝴蝶。
没有一丝风。石头也在出汗。
一丛低矮的野毛桃树缩成一团，
似乎只有它还在做梦。
这一切看上去都在某种秩序里——
以它反复的绝望的修剪声，
代替了所有清脆的鸟鸣。

Wang Jiaxin (王家新)

To Pushkin Monument in Shanghai

Like a stone, flung far from home,
standing on the crossroad,
we must go through a maze to reach it
after wandering around in a taxi.
We went in a drizzle; white smoke sizzles at food stands
around a small garden in the middle of the street.
Shanghai dialects that we don't understand
are heard bargaining...
My exiled poet, are you lonely?
On this rainy night, I can hardly see your prescient eyes,
the corners of your mouth like stone axes
but touching your moss-covered pedestal,
A burst of cold spreads through my body...
and now, I return to your side.
(wine bars have popped up on all sides)
My poet, are you still gazing forward?
How long will you stand there gazing?
Here in Shanghai, very few people know your name,
inscribed against tyrannical ruin and shrouded by prosperity.
Perhaps we should use keener Chinese
to make your name illustrious again;
Perhaps we should leave you to weeds.

Translated by Joan Xie

上海普希金纪念碑

像一尊飞来石，耸立在
一个远离故国的交叉路口，
第一次去寻觅它时，出租车
绕了很久，像是某种迷失
最终把我们带到这里；
我们去时，街心小花园四周的烧烤摊
在细雨中还冒着滋滋的白烟，
人们以我们听不懂的上海话
问着价钱……
流亡的诗人，你孤独吗？
雨夜，我无法看清你那远望的眼睛
和石斧般的嘴角，
我只能用手触摸布满青苔的基座，
任一阵冰凉传遍全身……
而现在，我再次回到你的身边
（四周的酒吧也多了起来）
诗人，你仍在那里眺望吗
你还要眺望多久？
这里是上海，很少有人知道
你那被繁华掩盖的
刻在专制废墟上的名字，
也许，我们只能用更锋锐的汉语
才能再次把它擦亮。
也许，我们只能任其荒芜。

Wang Jiaxin (王家新)

The Street

I shall not return my borrowed dust
to the earth...
—Mandelstam

1
After years of turbulence,
I now have a street—a narrow one in a residential neighborhood,
a treed one where we've lived for five years,
a small one that is still waiting for the swallow
from my childhood and the butterfly from Mandelstam.

2
Every day I walk on this street, in the golden sunset,
or at cicada green summer noon.
Even in the middle of writing, I can't help
But look at the street from my window
as if it were indispensable white space
between two lines of verse.

3
Now, a girl in a short skirt walks by, and I wish
that her brisk steps stand still
on a Grecian urn, or at least slow down to
let me take a good look at her from Du Fu's eyes,
or reach out to her for Yeats' hands.

4
Along this street, I buy daily bread and green vegetables
sometimes for my rabbit.
Oh, the hot steam from the "Hangzhou Xiaolongbao."
and children's joyful noises in that kindergarten
I like them as I like the silence
when school is closed: eternal quiet childhood.

这条街

我将不向大地归还
我借来的尘土……
——曼德尔施塔姆

1
在多年的动荡生活之后，
我也有了一条街，一条夹在居民区的小街，
一条我们已居住了五年的绿荫小街，
一条仍在等待我童年的燕子
和曼德尔施塔姆的蝴蝶的小街。

2
这条街，每天我都下楼走一走，在金色的黄昏，
或是伴着夏日蝉鸣的绿色正午，
即使在写作的时候我也往往忍不住
望一眼窗外的这条街，好像它就是
两行诗之间不能缺少的空白。

3
现在，一个穿短裙的少女走过，而我希望
她轻快的移动就是静止，
就像永远走在希腊古瓮上的画里，
至少走慢一点，我要替杜甫他老人家多看她一眼，
我还想替老叶芝向她伸出手来。

4
就是沿着这条街，我买来每天的面包、青菜，
（有时则专门去给我们家的兔子买吃的）
哦，街头那家“杭州小笼包”揭锅时的热气！
还有那家幼儿园，我喜欢孩子们的尖叫如同我喜欢
放学后的安静：那永恒的寂静的童年。

5
One unforgettable spring, (which year?)
right outside the neighborhood,
peach flowers blossomed on an iron fence,
only for three days, like a dream.
Ever since my time at hard labor,
pink clouds float before my eyes,
just float, even on a smoggy day.

6
Squatting mechanic, express mail courier, leaflet distributor…
I salute them all, and more,
when a funeral procession passes the street every year,
drumming and gonging, I drag my son
to watch by the window,
just like watching the other side of the moon.

7
Nightfall, the street bakes with a good smell of sweet potatoes.
("no roasted chestnuts on the streets of Paris," Paul Éluard once said)
Noon, electric pole stretches its shadow.
In the early summer, old banyan trees show fragrant flowers,
after an autumn rain, leaves golden on ginkgo trees!

8
Sometimes I bury myself in writing, never go downstairs,
but the street is still there. I open the curtain, ah, it's snowing—
At that moment, God saves us.
Even our family rabbit, at that moment
sits awed with me by the window for a long time.

9
We're renting here for my son's school,
but I love the street.
I love the fourth-floor window (not too high or too low)
love four seasons rotating, love its light and shadows.
It has dyed my soul its full colors.

5
难忘的春天（那是哪一年？），似乎一步出小区，
街边铁栅栏内的桃花就绽开了，
梦幻般的，虽然只开了三天，
从此我这个苦役犯的眼前就飘着几朵彩云，
就飘着，哪怕是在雾霾天。

6
蹲着的修车匠，飞窜的快递员，站着发小广告的……
我向这一切致敬，不仅如此，
每年这条街上还走过敲锣打鼓送葬的行列，
每到那时，我就拉着儿子来到窗边，
好像是让他观看月球的另一面。

7
傍晚，街头烤红薯的糊香味。
（“巴黎的大街上没有烤栗子吃了”，艾吕雅）
正午，电线杆拉长的阴影。
初夏时分，老槐树洒下的馨香细碎花蕊，
一场场秋雨后，银杏树那金币般的叶子！

8
有时我一连数日埋头写作，不曾下楼，
但那条街仍在那里，拉开窗帘，啊，下雪了——
那一瞬，好像就是上苍对我们的拯救！
那一瞬，连我们家的小兔子，也和我一起
久久地伫立在窗前。

9
就是这条街，虽然它并非我们自己的家，
我们只是为了孩子上学在这里租住，
但我爱这条街，爱这四楼上的窗户（它不高也不低），
爱街上的一年四季，爱它的光与影，
我的灵魂已带上了它们的颜色。

10
And the breeze on the street
greets my brow gently with every sleepwalk,
reconciling me with life. On a hot day,
it seems to carry me to Qingdao or Dalian—
Sea and sail just around the corner of the street.

11
Yes, I love this street. I settle down
and live again on "borrowed dust."
On the night of my birthday, I wandered the street,
less than 500 meters, back and forth three times:
followed by a tear-jerking star.

12
I love this street. From here I see the distant mountain
(not yet blocked by tall buildings)—Beijing Xishan.
I love that black silhouette against burned-out dusk
and the first headlight of a car at the end of the street
driving toward me from the boundaries of the soul.

13
This nameless street (you've read this poem and still won't find it),
facing it, I translated Mandelstam
who never could settle down, died in exile
and hoped that the "Moslem-butterfly" would survive his death—
survive to fly back to that country, to that street.

14
And "that street" is also "this street," just as
"this street" will become "that street"—
Next year we will move after our son graduates from elementary school
but I will visit the street many years later, so will our child—
So will the swallow from my childhood.

Translated by Joan Xie

10
还有这街上的微风！每次梦游般出去时，
它就会徐徐拂来问候我的眉头。
它一次次使我与生活和解。而在闷热天，
它则好像把我带向了青岛或大连——
一拐过这条街口，就是大海与帆！

11
是的，我爱这条街，它使我安顿下来，
使我靠“借来的尘土”再活一次。
过生日的那晚，我想在这条街上一直走下去，
但它还不到五百米，我就来回走了三趟：
伴着天上的那颗让我流泪的小星。

12
而我爱这条街，还因为可看到远山（幸好它没有
被高楼完全挡住）——那是北京西山；
我爱它在黄昏燃尽后的黑色剪影，
爱街的尽头第一辆亮起的雪亮车灯，
它好像就从灵魂的边界向我驶来。

13
就是这条无名小街（你读了这首诗也找不到它），
就是面对它，我翻译了曼德尔施塔姆，
他居无定所，死于流放，却希望在他死后
那只“白色粉蝶”能在它的跨距间活着——
飞回到那个国度，飞回到那条街。

14
而“那条街”也就是“这条街”，正如
“这条街” 也将变成 “那条街”——
明年我们的孩子小学毕业，我们也将搬走，
但多少年后我会重访这里，我们的孩子也会——
我童年的燕子也许会跟着他一起到来。

Wang Xiaoni (王小妮)

To the Rusty Sewage Pipe

I see only a rusted leg
Curled up pipeline on the ground.
Maybe it's too tired.
To stand firm
The single ever bending leg
Stretches his invisible body
Tightly in the dark.

Too many flickering lights
Too much congealed grease.
The iron coolie will fall
Silently
Leaving this crowded city short
One who does the dirty work.

Translated by Daniel Tay

致锈掉的下水道

我只看见一条锈掉的腿。
那蜷伏在地的管道
可能是太累了。
为了还能站稳
一直曲着的独腿
他无形的身体在暗处绷得正紧。

太多闪跳的灯
太多凝住不流的油。
铁打的苦力就要栽倒
无声无响地
这闹市又将少一个专做脏活儿的。

Wang Xiaoni (王小妮)

To the Sunlight in the Room

Right on time, it infiltrates my territory,
half the table receiving its sunshine.
Inventor of happiness, this tenured professor has come again.

Emanating warm yellow placebos
is the visiting sun's sole purpose.
And on its heels,
in this year, the ripe fruits, cotton and grains, blooming flowers,
oo la la, the earth is plump and bustling, full of luster.
But those in the very back,
those countless sweating, coughing, wheezing, chapped—
do not think they're invisible.

I refuse to be bathed again.
Winter light quivers, I don't deserve that light.

Translated by Daniel Tay

致屋子里的阳光

准时侵入我的地盘
半边桌子正接受它的照耀。
快乐的发明者，这终身教授又来了。

发放温黄的安慰剂
太阳到访的唯一目的。
紧跟其后的，正是
这一年里成熟的花朵果子棉桃和粮食
呼啦啦，大地丰盈热闹满是光泽。
可是，谁在后面的后面
无数流汗的咳嗽的气喘的皮肤龟裂的
不要以为看不见。

拒绝再被沐浴。
冬天的光亮有点抖，我不配享受那光。

Wang Xiaoni (王小妮)

To the Night of Thunderstorms

Blackout night, ten thousand things lose their voices.
Hiding at home, I ride out this demon weather, wait out its tricks,
wait for its dissolution after it has played.

Watch sound and light devastate the scene.
The sound of thunder passes, along the walls many pallid faces glow—
this is a flashback—legend says in the crow's previous life
her plume was pure as jade.

In the jolting lightning walking about,
I traverse the crow's stomach for a sleeping pill,
the road as dark as dark can get.
Using the eyeballs of birds to glimpse this impetuous world
this world in which cowards rejoice
vast and mighty.
Ambushed on all four sides, even in the darkest places heroes cannot hide.

Translated by Daniel Tay

致雷暴之夜

断电的晚上，万物失声。
躲在家里捱过这鬼天气，等它的把戏玩完
等它尽兴后的解散。

看这场声光电的蹂躏
雷声一过，四壁透出多张惨白的脸。
这就是倒叙，乌鸦传说中的前世
它的羽毛曾经纯洁如玉。

在闪电的跳窜里走动
穿过乌鸦的肚子去取一粒安眠药
这一路要多黑有多黑。
用飞禽的眼珠扫一眼这狂躁的世界
胆小鬼欢腾的世界
浩浩荡荡
四面都是埋伏，最暗处也躲不住英雄。

Wang Xiaoni (王小妮)

To Beijing in Goose Feather Snow

Of its own mind it's begun to snow
A piece of pure white land
is dressing itself up of its own mind.

Even flying to the clouds, you cannot touch the snow.
This beauty
The earth has closed down.
Circling planes are guardian angels of the city.

The good snow full of sky is diligently busying.
How many white livestock hand over their fur
Begrudging nothing
Molding humanity anew, building a city anew.

Translated by Daniel Tay

致鹅毛大雪中的北京

它竟然自顾自下雪了
洁白得出了奇的一片大地
自顾自地装扮着自己。

即使飞到它的头顶也无法接近它
这个美人
大地关闭了。
盘旋的飞机们都是护城的天使。

漫天的好雪，正闷头忙着。
多少白牲灵交出皮毛
没什么可吝惜的
重新捏出人，重新筑一座城。

Wang Xiaoni (王小妮)

To the Chimney on the Outskirts of Beijing

The most deserted place in the sky
The massive chimney spits thick smoke.
Loquacious curly black hair
The northern girl's sturdy braid.
Thick and flowing,
it madly whips,
Cinderella in a fit of rage.

No one can persuade her to return home
The cement chimney is her despot father.
Wrath is pushing her to run toward an even larger silver screen
Does she wish to stand?
Does she dare destroy the sky?

Translated by Daniel Tay

致京郊的烟囱

天上最空荡的地方
高大的烟囱正喷出浓烟。
滔滔不绝的黑卷发
北方姑娘那根粗壮的独辫子。
浓密又翻滚
蛮不讲理地甩出去
正在气头上的灰姑娘。

谁也不能说服她回家
那恶霸一样的水泥烟囱是她爸爸。
愤怒在推她，跑向更大的灰幕
她要站起来吗
她这是要顶破天吗。

Wang Xiaoni (王小妮)

Our Dusk

From behind, dusk shines on the man sitting in his office.

Dusk makes his two ears quite thin and red,
same as burnt, same as grilled,
same as hyperbole.

That half-transparent, natural jewelry
is the most beautiful thing on the human body.
It should not belong to us, it is nature's.

The sun sets
before the radiant knife leaves,
both left and right ears taken first.
Then the man taken away,
finally the knife has taken our dim yellow human world.

All the city streetlights promptly switch on,
crying and laughing,
all strenuously opening their newly lit mouths.

Translated by Daniel Tay

我们的傍晚

傍晚从背后照着那个坐在办公室的人。

傍晚使他的两只耳朵很薄又很红
烫的一样，烤的一样
经过夸张的一样。

那对半透明的自然的饰物
人类身上最好看的东西。
它不该属于我们，它是自然界的。

太阳落下去
光芒的刀在离开之前
先收走了左右两只耳朵。
后来收去人
最后一刀收尽了昏黄的人间。

全城的路灯准时打开
哭的和笑的
都努力张着他们忽然亮起来的嘴。

Wang Xiaoni (王小妮)

Cuckoo Clock

It sings out the time
It has briefly glimpsed all of us
Immediately backed into its little wooden house.
It's not stayed more than a moment.

In fear, it is captured by the giant craftsman
And lives in a pinewood cell.
It can never know its maker.
Everyone among us is a suspect.

Next is our turn, squeezed into time, locked up
Sunlight shining from a thousand years ago
Exerting ourselves sniffing daffodils that will flutter by the day after tomorrow.
Leaving in time, returning in time
Everything's been set.

Our hearts hold a paper garden
Propping up straight green bamboo
How unreal, how calm.
I arrogantly glance at the cuckoo clock
but have seen my kindred in this same dark place
As that poor figurine that shares its name with a grain drill.[11]
I won't dare be arrogant toward it again.

Translated by Daniel Tay

---

[11] In China, Cuckoo Bird is a brand of grain drill

布谷钟

它把时间报诵出来
它匆忙看了我们所有人一眼
立刻退回密闭的小木屋。
不多停留一刻。

它因为恐惧被巨大的工匠逮住
生活在松木造的牢笼
它不可能知道造它那人是谁。
我们中间的每一个都涉嫌。

下面轮到了我们，钻到时间里面，关紧闭
照着一千年以前的太阳
用力去闻闻后天才能飘过来的水仙味。
按时出门，按时归来
一切都设定好了。

我们心里似乎有座纸上花园
支撑一根挺直的青竹
多么不真实，多么镇定。
现在，我傲慢地瞄一眼布谷钟
我见到了暗处的同类
那个可怜的和播种机同名的木俑。
我再不敢傲慢了。

Wang Xiaoni (王小妮)

The Fish that Killed Itself

The moonlight's watered down.
A fish hurls itself out of the pond,
Lets out a few groans, stops moving.
Everything's grey, diluted.

I want to pick the newly blooming orchids
With that bolt upright scent
I've missed for a year.
I make a beeline for the blossoms
Run through a moonfield
And recklessly trample the fish that killed itself.

The fleshy mulberry leaves
The white bones jutting out
In the pearl of its little eye, a pool of light.
I recoil at once, completely forget the world's fragrant flowers.
Fish, oh fish, I'm so helpless.

Translated by Daniel Tay

自杀的鱼

月光松沓沓。
一条鱼猛一用劲跳出水池
哼了几声不动了。
四周发灰哦松沓沓。

想去摘朵新开的白兰
那香味笔直笔直
想了一年了。
直奔着花，跑过月亮地
不小心踩上这条自杀的鱼
软到吓人。

有肉的桑叶
白刺在起棱
小眼珠里一汪光。
赶紧后退，全忘了世上有花香
鱼哦鱼，我好无助。

Wang Yin (王寅)

In a Past Life I Was a Cobbler

In a past life I was a cobbler
His household was entered on the last line of a page in the city register
All of my desires and dreams
issued from his lips, blackened from years of clamping down on iron nails
lips like the dark roots of wheat beneath the earth
His eyes peered out from a cellar
fixed on the daily parade of leather shoes and riding boots
He imagined the warm calves beneath all those skirts
In a past life, like an amateur philosopher
close to the ground, hearing the sounds of the universe
listening to the way empty spaces swallow up the tides
listening to the way hurricanes lay waste to villages

In a past life I was a cobbler
I often see his smiling face in department store windows
moving toward me through a press of spirits, smiling
He left me not a silver mask
but raven hair and hands as strong as engines
He's a pair of ragged claws for my collection
a lottery ticket that's still unredeemed
a gale of shrill laughter aimed at the stars
The Revolution stirred him
but he was soon put to death by the immortal Emperor
His sopping wet head on a platter
he had to let curs lick the rain from his face

In a past life I was a cobbler
The greatest pressure I feel is to keep him from knowing
the pride and hatred I harbor towards him
In my stinking past life
I carried strings of shoes peeled from the feet of the living
which have meted out his secrets to me fitfully
Each time he faked his death and pretended to leave this world of dust
another iron nail would fall from his mouth

我的前生是一个补鞋匠

我的前生是一个补鞋匠
他的户籍在城市登记簿某一页的最后一行
我所有的情欲和幻想
全部来自他长年衔住铁钉而变得黝黑的嘴唇
这嘴唇犹如泥土之下麦子黑暗的根部
他探出地窖的双眼
天天盯住来来往往的皮鞋和马靴
想象着裙裾之中温暖的小腿
我的前生，像个业余哲学家
在贴近地面的地方更多地听到宇宙的声音
听到空洞如何吞噬潮汐
听到飓风如何毁灭村庄

我的前生是一个补鞋匠
我常常在百货公司的玻璃窗上看到他的笑容
他越过如此多拥挤的灵魂向着我微笑
他留给我的不是银面具
而是乌黑的头发和发动机般有力的双手
他是我珍藏中的一双干手爪
是未兑现的彩票号码
是向着星辰的一声凄厉狞笑
革命曾使他惊醒
但又很快被不朽的皇帝砍去头颅
他在盘子里湿淋淋的脑袋
只能任由野狗舔尽脸上的雨水

我的前生是一个补鞋匠
我最大的压抑是不让他知道
我对他怀有无限的自豪和仇恨
我的臭不可闻的前生
肩扛手提从活人脚上剥下的一串串鞋子
将他的秘密断断续续地传授给我
他每一次伪造他远离尘世的死亡
他的嘴里就会掉下一枚铁钉

I can only stay locked indoors and sit by the window
Watching an angry drunk and a housewife chase him down

In a past life I was a cobbler
His tailor friend is still a tailor
the kind-faced gardener is still a gardener
but each of them sits in his own marble bathtub
straight-backed and dignified like an aristocrat
perusing the morning paper at arms' length
Trailing the Red Planet on a summer day, riding a trolley that speeds toward
downtown
Beside me, people who toil in the heart of the city
pass through a diagonal slash to enter its bright, clean lowlands

(1993)

Translated by Andrea Lingenfelter

我只得锁在屋子里从窗帘后面
看他被愤怒的醉汉和主妇追逐

我的前生是一个补鞋匠
他的裁缝朋友今天依然是裁缝
慈眉善目的花匠依然是花匠
但他们在各自的大理石浴缸里
像威严的贵族那样腰背笔直
手臂平举，远远地端详早晨的报纸
只有我成了诗人，在一个早晨
尾随夏日的火星，乘坐一辆无轨电车驶向闹市中心
我的身边，城市中勤劳的人们
从倾斜的缺口进入这片明亮干净的低地

1993

首次发表：《王寅诗选》花城出版社 2005年

Wang Yin (王寅)

Louse on Idlers' Street

The louse on Idlers' Street
is like a madman eating cake, uncommonly nimble
in the driving rain
tripping down a winding arcade
Like the Revolution, like the news
it tells me the secret of destiny
its voice shaking my eardrums

Face coated in gold leaf
it keeps crossing its forelegs in a porcelain basin
and languidly blows clouds of smoke
Louse on Idlers' Street
its entire life a symbol
When at last it floats into a cup of coffee
its youthful face poised to drown
flashes a crafty smile
and follows that sunlit ark to Heaven

This enlightening creature, my only teacher
has always been a silent stone
which possesses nonetheless the loftiest of destinies

(1999)

Translated by Andrea Lingenfelter

闲人街上的虱子

闲人街上的虱子
就像食饼的疯子，肉体格外轻盈
在倾斜的暴风雨中
踮着脚走过门外的回廊
像革命，像新闻
它告诉我命运的秘密
它的声音震撼我的耳膜

脸上贴着金箔
在瓷盘上反复交叉着前腿
悠闲地吞云吐雾
闲人街上的虱子
它的一生就是一种象征
它最后飘浮在咖啡杯中的时候
行将溺死的青年的脸
闪现诡谲的笑容
跟随着这盛满阳光的方舟驶向天堂

这启迪我的生物，我惟一的教师
从来是沉默的石头
但却有着至高无上的命运

Wang Yin (王寅)

Men Out of Step with the Times

You tell me you miss those
slow paced days of the past
the equally leisurely pace of bicycles
and leaky wristwatches

We're both out of step with the times, lifting our old-fashioned cups of coffee
drinking a cup to Caroline, another to poverty
drinking a toast to the season of mental confusion
another to unrelenting snowfall
and another to the listening devices of yore
The last cup we drink is to ourselves
men out of step with the times

You should know how happy it makes me to imagine you
in an utterly unfamiliar city
like Jerusalem or Marrakesh, or Johnson, Vermont
or some other city whose name neither of us can pronounce
And some day when my head is in the clouds
I might happen to run into you on a rainy street

Thus, when I pause for a moment while writing you
it's just me with my head in the clouds again
As soon I send the email, that's when
the relentless wind and rain
come to a halt at last

(2015)

Translated by Andrea Lingenfelter

不合时宜的人

你对我说，怀念那些
缓慢的旧日子
同样缓慢的自行车
和漏水的手表

我们都是不合时宜的人，端着不合时宜的咖啡
这一杯敬卡洛琳，这一杯敬贫穷
这一杯敬神经错乱的季节
这一杯敬无休无止的雪
敬过时的窃听器
最后一杯敬我们自己
这些不合时宜的人

你该知道，我多么乐意想象你
在一个极其陌生的城市
譬如耶路撒冷 譬如马拉喀什
或者那些我们都念不出地名的城市
好让我在走神的时候
在被雨淋湿的街道上与你不期而遇

所以，给你写信停笔的时候
就是我一如既往地走神
我发送电子邮件的瞬间，就是
无休无止的暴风雨
终于停歇的时刻

2015

Xiao Xiao (潇潇)

Spring and Autumn Sonnets[12]

Gong: Vulaines-sur-Seine

On a Vulaines-sur-Seine afternoon
The Seine, where sunlight plays reed flutes
like a lake on the ends of the horizon flowing with ancient music
The sun sits in front of the door of Stéphane Mallarmé's former residence

Dear Xu Shuang rides in her saddle
taking us from Fontainebleau
to Pan's old house. At the corner of the second floor
my sleeve brushes away a few grains of old dust on the ladder

Mallarmé's Tuesday
falls into my poem this afternoon
"Dear, poems are written by language;
they aren't written using thought."

In this moment, Paris' March
is preparing a heavy snowstorm for an orphan

Shang: Clermont-Ferrand

At 2:10pm in the Media Library of Jaude,
the audience coming from the volcanic city takes their seats in succession
I get up and read poems for spring
Lily reads for me in volcanic-flavored French

Afterward, Puy de Dome's body grows heavier
merging with the color of the sky at dusk
Notre Dame's slender spire
pierces the night's grief and boundlessness

---

[12] Gong, Shang, Jue, Zhi, Yu are the pre-Tang names for the pentatonic scale, roughly corresponding to Do, Re, Mi, So, La.

春秋十四行

宫：维莱纳 苏尔 塞纳

维莱纳-苏尔-塞纳小镇的午后
吹奏芦笛的闪光的塞纳河
像天边的湖泊流淌着古乐
日头坐在马拉美故居的门前

亲爱的徐爽驾着她的坐骑
带我们从枫丹白露
到牧神的老房子，二楼的拐角
我的衣袖碰落扶梯上几粒旧尘

马拉美的星期二
在这个下午，落进我的诗里
“亲爱的，诗歌是语言写出来的
不是用思想写出来的”

此刻，巴黎的三月
为一个孤儿正准备着一场大雪

商：克莱蒙 费朗

下午两点十一分，在朗诺图书馆
来自火山城的听众陆续入座
我起身，为春天读诗
莉莉用火山味道的法语为我朗读

之后，多姆山的身子越来越沉
与旁晚昏暗的天色融为一体
圣母教堂细长的尖顶
刺破黑夜无边的忧伤和苍茫

Life is just an appointment with death
We come to the castle born in 1513
The face of the aged wood door has rhombus-shaped iron nails growing all over it

The flickering candle, the despondent fireplace. Red wine
leads people to fall into the river of love. I'm at the cellar entrance; it says
you're just a sojourner in my body.

Jue: Aigues-Mortes

This is Aigues-Mortes commune
To the left, about 30 kilometers to Montpellier
In the Mediterranean bay, it is like a cyclamen saying good-bye

On an old street, we walk through an ancient spring,
pass through an ancient city gate, travel a few ancient meters
A pair of mallards are whispering in the reeds

The 3pm sunlight is scalding
The scent of the Mediterranean floats up
The ancient pier that welcomed and sent off the Crusaders
is like a gold ear listening to the distance

The knotgrass is producing berries on the vine, ripening to black and purple
like the congealed blood of histories' numerous battles

The tragedies that can be described aren't the cruelest
The sorrows that can be wept for aren't fatal

Zhi: Rennes

Rennes at nightfall is like a sexy gentleman
infatuating so many Far Eastern women

This time, Rennes in March
paused for us on a boat on the Seine

人生下来就是与死亡相约
我们来到1513年出生的古堡
苍老的木门脸上，长满菱形铁钉的雀斑

幽明的蜡烛，抑郁的壁炉。红酒
让人坠入爱河。我在地窖入口，它说
你只是我身体里的一个过客

角：艾格 莫特

这是艾格-莫特小城
向左，距离蒙彼利埃30多公里
在地中海湾像一朵告别的仙客来

我们在老街，走过古老的春天
穿过古老的城门，行脚古老的几米
一对野鸭在芦苇间窃窃私语

下午3点的阳光，滚烫
地中海的味道飘浮起来
当年迎送十字军东征的古城墙垛
像一只只金色的耳朵，聆听着遥远

蚂蚁草在藤蔓上结着浆果，成熟紫黑
像历史上一次次战争，凝固的血

能够描述的惨烈不是最惨的
可以痛哭的悲伤不是致命的

徵：雷恩

入夜的雷恩像性感的绅士
让多少远东的少女成为花痴

这一次，三月的雷恩
在塞纳河的船上为我们停顿

Onstage, Chantal's precise, passionate French
made me ache again and fall into the poetry
as if she and I had floated to the edge of darkness
The transparent grief in her eyes tumbled down drop by drop

Just then, the pain that had accumulated inside me for so long commanded me
to recite and dance in Europe's spring. They empathized
with humiliation and bitterness coming from the East

It was on this day that the striking crowds on the street came over,
escorted by cops on motorcycles, like a holiday parade
If this was in the Far East, something major would happen for sure

***Yu*: Angers**

I arrive in Angers in the wild rain
My heart lands in this relaxed place
A thirteenth century castle
rigidly secured, on the bank of Loire River

Today it's open to tourists
as if to verify both sides of the world

On the tapestry, thousands of flowers burst forth humanity's doomsday
The Apocalypse embroiders God's illumination,
but most of the time people are covering their ears

The castle has become a stone prison
The prisoners' freedoms are the length of the fetters and chains
I walk into the prison cell; cold germinates from the top of my head

Angers, Angers, just now in Kyoto, in my mind
in the torrential rain, you're floating, drifting

Translated by Jami Proctor Xu

舞台上，尚德兰精准、动情的法语
再一次让我在诗歌中疼痛下坠
仿佛我与她一起飘到黑暗的边缘
她眼里透明的忧伤，一滴滴滚落

此刻，积蓄已久的苦难命令我
在欧洲的春天朗读舞蹈，来自东方的
耻辱和酸楚，他们感同身受

就在这一天，罢工人群从街道走来
摩托警车护送着秩序，像节日的游行
如果在远东，肯定出大事了

羽：昂热

我来了，昂热在乱纷纷的雨里
我的心在松弛地降落
十三世纪的城堡
密不透风的森严，卢瓦尔河畔

今天对游人开放
似乎在正反面印证世界

挂毯上千枝花绽开人类的末日
启示录刺绣着神的启示
而人们更多的时候是捂着耳朵

城堡变成石头的监狱
囚犯的自由是镣铐铁链的长度
我走进牢房，寒冷在头顶发芽

昂热，昂热，此刻在京都，在我心中
倾盆的大雨里，你飘浮着，漂浮着

Xiao Xiao (潇潇)

The Seoul in My Heart

Seoul in my heart
isn't a nation's capital
like Beijing, Tokyo, or Hanseong

Seoul is my lover from abroad—
its glistening tenderness takes over the senses
slightly aloof and a little shy

In Insadong, every
curved and winding tiny street, flower,
plant, and poet's bar—
heaven, street artist, traveler

gently attracts me
with the brief warm encounters I have with them
as if the love my heart has treasured
for many years gives off the scent of eaglewood incense

Translated by Jami Proctor Xu

首尔在我心里

首尔，在我心里
不是一个国家的首都
比如北京，东京，汉城

首尔是我异国他乡的情人
扑面而来的亮晶晶的温存
还有一些矜持和一点害羞

仁寺洞的每一条
弯弯拐拐的小街，花草
植物，诗人酒吧——
归天，路边艺人、过客

与我擦肩而过的小温暖
轻轻地吸引着我
像内心珍藏了多年的
一段恋情，散发出沉香

Xiao Xiao (潇潇)

West Lake, Mirror of the Soul

That day
when the boat approached the Three Ponds,
it began to drizzle gently

The lotus leaves of the whole lake began rocking
large and tiny droplets

At the top of the stone pagoda
an egret was fully focused on
using its beak to comb
the rolling raindrops on its feathers

The tranquil, peaceful auspiciousness of its world
Its pure, lonely appearance

along with our noisy cameras,
shallow online likes, and exclamations
formed a scene from *Pride and Prejudice*

The disturbance of our impropriety
The egret flapped its wings
brushed off the unwanted moods from its body
and flew away

Beneath the lake's surface, the fragrance of plum blossom piles
gently rippled out

Translated by Jami Proctor Xu

西湖，灵魂的一面镜子

那一天
泛舟靠近三潭的时候
小雨开始飘落

满湖的荷叶摇晃着
大大小小的水珠

石塔的尖顶上
一只白鹭心无旁骛
用嘴壳梳理羽毛上
滚动的珠子

它世界的宁静、祥和
纯粹，孤单的样子

与我们喧嚣的镜头
肤浅的点赞、惊叹
形成一幅傲慢与偏见的画面

我们不知分寸的打扰
白鹭拍拍翅膀
拍落一身的不情愿
飞走了

湖面下轻轻荡起
梅花桩松木的香气

Yang Ke (杨克)

This Is the Latest on Yang Ke

He eats a pepper steak in a pub
then "grabs a cab" as they say in this town, then
wanders past stalls piled sky-high with color.
Here in the South where night never falls
He watches money counterfeit love with female strangers—
His heart is half rotted away by now.

Once in awhile from a jumble of icily intelligent words known as poetry
he looks up
like a fly on its pile of rubbish.

Translated by Simon Patten

杨克的当下状态

在啤酒屋吃一份黑椒牛扒
然后“打的”，然后
走过花花绿绿的地摊。
在没有黑夜的南方
目睹金钱和不相识的女孩虚构爱情
他的内心有一半已经陈腐。

偶尔，从一堆叫做诗的冰雪聪明的文字
伸出头来
像一只蹲在垃圾上的苍蝇。

Yang Ke (杨克)

The Chinese People

Those migrant workers forced to demand their wages.
148 pairs of battered hands
held out from Daping's caved-in mine.
Li Aiye, who caught AIDS after giving blood.
The shepherd bachelors of the loess slopes.
Gossipy women licking a finger to count money.
Hair salon girls: unlicensed sex-workers.
Peddlers engaged in a running battle with city authorities.
Old bosses
in need of a sauna.

The 9 to 5 tribe off to work on their bicycles.
Idlers with no where to go and nothing to do.
The bar-room wasters. Old men
sipping tea as they pet songbirds.
Scholars who fill the heads of their listeners with fog.
Derros, punters, porters stinking to high heaven;
dandies, beggars, doctors, secretaries (and secret mistresses into the bargain);
workplace clowns
and other supporting actors.

From the Avenue of Heavenly Peace to the Guangzhou Road
I have yet to see "the Chinese people" this winter;
I've seen ordinary, speaking bodies
keeping each other warm
on buses day after day.
They're like grimy coins:
their users hand them over frowning
to society.

Translated by Simon Patten

人民

那些讨薪的民工。那些从大平煤窑里伸出的
148双残损的手掌。
卖血染上艾滋的李爱叶。
黄土高坡放羊的光棍。
沾着口水数钱的长舌妇。
发廊妹，不合法的性工作者。
跟城管打游击战的小贩。
需要桑拿的
小老板。

那些骑自行车的上班族。
无所事事的溜达者
那些酒吧里的浪荡子。边喝茶
边逗鸟的老翁。
让人一头雾水的学者。
那臭烘烘的酒鬼、赌徒、挑夫
推销员、庄稼汉、教师、士兵
公子哥儿、乞丐、医生、秘书（以及小蜜）
单位里头的丑角或
配角。

从长安街到广州大道
这个冬天我从未遇到过“人民”
只看见无数卑微地说话的身体
每天坐在公共汽车上
互相取暖。
就像肮脏的零钱
使用的人，皱着眉头，把他们递给了，社会。

Yang Ke (杨克)

Daylight Savings

Ahead of time trains depart
Ahead of time girls mature
Ahead of time birthday candles are blown out
And in a well-planned murder
A knife goes in white
And comes out red
Ahead of time

Yet chicks refuse to crack their shell
The moon fails to light the night sky

Yet a realist writer jogging in the morning street
Has been killed by the first bus
Which was running off schedule
So black humor and the absurdist school
Can at last be understood

And the guy going for a date in the old place
At the old time has met another girl
The deceased—having just been cremated—
Has the wrong time listed on his death certificate
And men stand bewildered over the theft
Of an hour of sun and air
Is time fair?

Translated by Denis Mair

夏时制

火车提前开走
少女提前成熟
插在生日蛋糕上的蜡烛
提前吹灭
精心策划的谋杀案
白刀子提前进去
红刀子提前出来

只是孵房的小鸡拒绝出壳
只是入夜时分
月光不白

马路上晨跑的写实作家
在本来无车的时刻
被头班车撞死　理解了
黑色幽默和荒诞派
老地点老时间赴约会的小伙
从此遇上另一个女孩
躺在火葬场的死者
享年徒有虚名
莫名其妙被窃走一小时阳光空气
一个个目瞪口呆

时间是公正的么?

Yang Ke (杨克)

Windy Beijing

Windy Beijing:
people on bikes
and startled sparrows everywhere
The air is filthy
The sun, trapped in haze,
is like a ruddy moon
Yesterday, only yesterday, we had clear autumn weather
Air-borne paper   metaphysical, soaring
Plastic bags glide overhead   swollen
so that I see the shape of the wind.
Leaves rustle in trees
Covered from head to foot in dust, sparrows
fly twittering back to their nests
The ground is covered with Beijing accents
Thou, in whose unseen presence the buses and taxis
are driven
Riding my bike, I
like an arrow
taut against the bow-string
Fired into the Beijing wind
I shoot through the door of my rented house
Two policemen come knocking:
I remember my boyhood,
reaching into a nest beneath a roof

Translated by Denis Mair

风中的北京

风中的北京
骑自行车的人
四下惊飞的麻雀

发粘的空气很脏
陷在灰蒙蒙里的太阳
像一圈暗红的月亮

昨天　昨天还秋高气爽

翻飞的纸　形而上飞翔的纸
掠过头顶的塑料袋　鼓胀的塑料袋
使我看清了风的形状

树叶在响
灰头土脸的麻雀
吱吱喳喳回巢的麻雀

洒落一地京腔

风吹人低见车辆

骑自行车的我
像一支箭
紧绷在弓弦上

射进北京的风里
射入租的家门

两个敲门的警察
令我忆起少年屋檐下
我伸进鸟窝的两根手指

Yang Ke (杨克)

Nowadays High-Rises Are the Crops of the City

Vying for land with rice   vying for land with corn
Vying for land with soybeans and sorghum
Vying for land with folks who dwell in old buildings
Nowadays high-rises are the crops of the city

Rice plants in rural villages get shorter all the time
Old people and children
Are the last two straggly crops
Shaken, shriveled parents, a temporary shortage of children
The city cuts deep furrows   strews seeds across them
Buildings spring up like stalks, adding height each day
Balconies, penthouses, landscaped estates out your window
Greenery ready to flower, brought in half-grown from nurseries

The soil belongs to the state   the state belongs to the people
But the high and mighty state seems to have no handle on the soil
It seems unrelated to those myrmidons who are busy filling their bellies
Thunk! A big seal stamped on a document who-knows-where
Sets the snowball of wealth rolling for certain people
The developer signs for rights to a really big plot
   with borrowed funds he can hire workers to till it
Skillful planting is still done by farmers as day labor or contract
Now they have donned hard hats
Grain prices keep climbing   agencies and brokers rake in cash
On the escalator of merit   big cash always wins promotions
The city's crops block out sun and sky
Swarms of people undulate among the roots, on foot and wheels
Like leeches, earthworms and tadpoles
We like to say land is measured in gold
How grand these gold-plated houses as thick as comb's teeth
Where common people can't even afford a snail-shell abode!

Those who face gentrification watch over ancestral paddies
A high wind is blowing in the sky as the economy slumps
On Weibo, land developers complain to high heaven
All day with tireless zeal they till this field of new hope

Translated by Denis Mair

如今高楼大厦是城里的庄稼

跟水稻争地，跟玉米争地
跟黄豆红高粱争地
跟住在老宅里的男女老幼争地
如今高楼大厦是城里的庄稼

乡村的农作物越种越矮
老人和儿童
是最后两棵痛疼的庄稼
摇晃干瘪的父母，青黄不接的子女
城市深耕直播
建筑日夜拔节，愈长愈高
阳台、顶层和入户花园
又嫁接绿叶和开花的植物

土地是国家的，国家是人民的
可似乎并不被高高在上的国家掌控
也跟为口腹忙碌的蚁民无关
一枚大印在暗地里把几个人的商机
盖得皇天浩荡
开发商是承包大户，贷款雇人耕种
种植能手依旧是农民，那些长工短工
戴上工人的安全帽
粮食不断涨价，政府和商人赚个盆满钵满
财富和政绩芝麻开花节节高

城市的庄稼遮天蔽日
行人和汽车穿行在密密麻麻的根部
像水蛭、蚯蚓和蝌蚪
多么好啊，一寸土地一寸金
种出的黄金屋鳞次栉比
让多少老百姓住不起蜗居

被拆迁者死命守护祖宗的矮脚稻
高天也刮起大风，可经济又倒伏
在另一片虚拟的土地上
几个大房地产商，在微博叫苦连天
他们每天都勤勤恳恳，耕耘这新的希望的田野

Yang Ke (杨克)

Guangzhou

In China, for good fortune, go to Guangzhou.
—Proverb

From north to south, our People's Boulevard leads heavenward
A train's direction is the direction of fate
Innocent beyond description, excited faces
Show the genuine face of my motherland

Travelers stagger across the station plaza
Colliding like birds that strayed indoors
Worn out or not, who would shun this City of Flowers and Grain?
How I envy those well dressed folks   fitting into conventional life
Like sunbeams between transparent panes
Imagine the sound of a counting machine, riffling paper bills
This era's most marvelous music, and someone always gets to hear it
Always some people's desires bloom ten thousand purples and reds
Countless folks vanish along the way to Pearl Delta
Another cloudburst is absorbed into the soil
But some people are stuck in a prolonged delirium
They suffer from the beginning right through to the end
Once again their train's direction will be the direction of fate

Translated by Denis Mair

广州

东西南北中，发财到广东。
——民谣

由北向南，我的人民大道通天
列车的方向就是命运的方向
纯朴的莫名兴奋的脸
呈现祖国更真实的面容

盲目的漫游者，在车站广场
误入房间的鸟惊慌碰撞
不管多么疲乏，也不愿逃离这鲜花稻穗之城
嫉羡那衣冠楚楚的大俗的人
像阳光在透明的玻璃中间飞翔

想象点钞机翻动大额钞票的声响
这个年代最美妙动听的音乐，总有人能听到
总有人的欲望可以万紫千红地开花
走向珠江三角洲，无数的人就这样消失
一场暴雨被土地吸收

也有人只是经历了漫长的白日梦
开始是苦难，结束也是苦难
列车的方向再度是命运的方向

Yao Feng (姚风)

Sunshine, 21st June

June 21st is a lonely day
a breeze brings jacaranda blossoms to their fate

a no.18 tram, carrying passengers I don't know
dawdles at the terminus

where I sit alone on a bench
bathing in the sunshine of June 21st

then in my loins, heat
as if a hand descended along my body
and that's when I see
all the fallen flowers fly back to their branches

Translated by Kit Kelen, Karen Kun, Penny Fang Xia

6月21日的陽光

這一天，孤獨的品質很好
藍花楹隨風飄向宿命
18路有軌電車，載著我不相識的乘客
緩緩抵達終點

我獨自坐在終點的長椅上
沐浴6月21日的陽光

突然，我感到腰間一片灼熱
彷彿有一隻手在我身上降落，把我撫摸
我看見
滿地的落花都飛回了樹枝

In Kyoto

in Kyoto, I feel as if I were back in the Tang Dynasty
I noted kanji in your language
some of which look even better
than the Chinese original
Yoshino, Arashiyama, Sasa-yuri...
we have similar features
but you are not me, I am not you
take for instance the Guanyin at Kiyomizu Temple
just as kind and decent as any we have in China
but conveys
the local spirit of Japan
or the magnolias on the hillside
like magnolias I saw in Beijing
but when a breeze blows, you will hear
the clatter of clogs in the rustle of leaves
a young lady in kimono minces over
pretty, shy, gentle
sakura blossom drifts onto her jade black bun
but I can't fall in love with this place
can't even feel a shred of pride
passing through the noren curtain into a bar
a dish of delicately prepared Japanese tofu
alerts all five senses
to this country
I must respect

Translated by Kit Kelen, Karen Kun, Penny Fang Xia

在京都

在京都，我彷彿回到唐朝
我認識你的一些字，甚至看到更好看的漢字：
吉野、嵐山、百合……
你的五官也和我相似
但你不是我，我也不是你
就像清水寺的觀音，一樣的端莊慈祥
但眉宇間凝聚的
是日本的晴空和山嵐
就如同這山坡上的玉蘭
看似與北京的玉蘭毫無異樣
但風一吹，我就聽到
簌簌聲中傳來木屐的聲響
一個身穿和服的女子姍姍走來
美麗，嬌羞，溫柔
櫻花飄零， 落在你黑玉似的發簪
然而，在此我始終無法熱愛
但也沒有一絲的驕傲
在青布掩映的小酒館，一塊精心調製的豆腐
也讓我五味雜陳
對這個國家，我不得不心懷敬意

Gravestone of Su Xiaoxiao[13]

you arc the only one buried beside the
bridge
people crowd above, you are peacefully sleeping
you have loved and now love no one

the sunset dyes West Lake
a jug
of vintage Nu'er Hong[14]
how many daughters to marry off!

we, a party of drunk men
vie for pictures in front of your grave

but who among us
dares a big red big green wedding with you?

Translated by Kit Kelen, Karen Kun, Penny Fang Xia

---

[13] Su Xiaoxiao, with her great beauty and intelligence, was known as a talented courtesan and poet in the Southern Qi. She refused to marry for wealth.
[14] Literally "red girl," Nu'er Hong is a fine rice wine

蘇小小墓

你是唯一葬在橋頭的
人群熙熙攘攘，你靜默地睡著
或者醒著
你已愛過，現在誰也不愛

夕陽下的西湖，是一壇陳年女兒紅
多少女兒出嫁了

我們一行男人，趁著酒興
爭先與你合影

只是合影中這些男人
誰敢大紅大綠地娶你

Yao Feng (姚风)

Two Axes in an Art Gallery

axes not only chop wood
but also loot and lop off heads
lumberjacks, executioners, axe gangs and revolutionaries
Li Kui, Li Gui,
a demolition crew…
all in different social situations
in different historical moments
take up the axe
even that delicate poet, Gu Cheng

yesterday when I visited an art gallery
I saw an axe
which had broken another axe's handle
it was leaning arrogantly on the wall
leering down at me
as I passed by

Translated by Kit Kelen, Karen Kun, Penny Fang Xia

在美術館看見兩把斧子

斧子，既可伐木劈柴
也可打家劫舍，也可砍掉頭顱
伐木工人、劊子手、斧頭幫、革命者、
李逵、李鬼，或者拆遷隊……
在不同的社會
在不同的歷史時刻
都舉起了斧子
甚至弱不禁風的顧城

昨天在MOU美術館
我看見一把斧子
砍斷了另外一把斧子的木柄
並趾高氣昂地靠著牆
打量著
正在走過的我

Yao Feng (姚风)

God

on the flight to San Francisco
I sat beside an American couple
they were about sixty years old
they were bringing back a babbling Chinese infant
who had never flown before
he was curious at first, then burst into tears
when the plane took off
he was staring blankly, pulling and scratching at the couple
it turns out he was a blind child

it was a long journey and out of curiosity
I had a chat with them
I learned that they had come to China
to adopt this abandoned blind boy
'but he can't see!' I blurted out
thinking the way Chinese people do
they said 'we know, but we wanted to do this
to let him know that he is loved'

the plane continued in the blue sky, at fifteen thousand meters
the shame I felt like a dark abyss
I have to admit: I am not so philanthropic
for devout Christians
the code of conduct
has to do with belief and atonement
but I can't attribute their benevolence to God
In my opinion, this couple is God

now I am sitting beside God
but I am so far away from God
so far

Translated by Kit Kelen, Karen Kun, Penny Fang Xia

上帝

在飛往三藩市的班機上
我身邊坐著一對美國夫婦
年紀大約六十來歲
帶著一個牙牙學語的中國男孩
他是第一次坐飛機
先是好奇，起飛時卻大哭起來
眼神茫然地在美國夫婦身上又抓又扯
原來，他是個瞎孩子

旅途漫長，我好奇地
和美國夫婦閒聊
才知道他們專程來到中國
就是為了收養這個被遺棄的瞎孩子
「可，可他什麼都看不見啊！」
按照中國人慣常思維，我本能地說到
「我們知道，但我們喜歡就樣做，
讓他知道還有人愛他。」

飛機在一萬五千米的藍天飛行
我卻羞愧地向著黑暗的深淵墜落
必須承認：我沒有如此大愛
或許有人會說，他們是虔誠的基督徒
信仰與贖罪
是他們行為方式的準則
但我不願把他們的仁慈歸功於上帝
在我看來，他們就是上帝
現在我就坐在上帝的身邊
但我距離上帝是如此遙遠
如此遙遠

Yen Ai-Lin (颜艾琳)

Barcode

You must be simple.
You must be uncanny.
But, at the same time, you must be knowable,
and obscure.

You are the living tombstones of identity,
runes of price,
a tiny monetary dictionary
hidden inside ten thousand beings,
waiting to go through the checkout counter,
to be deciphered into one smoky language.

Translated by Jonathan Chiang

条形码

你必须是简单的。
你必须是神秘的。
但，又必须是可知的、
难以一语道破；

你是身份的生之墓碑、以及
价值的灵符、
一部小小的金钱字典，
隐藏在万物的体内，
随时等待通过收款机
译码出轻烟似的语言。

Yen Ai-Lin (颜艾琳)

Geeky Girl's Room

They say, I stare at the screen dumb as a doorknob
They say, like firewood I'm skinny and scrawny
They say, I stammer and slur when I talk
They say, my name is Geeky Girl

But they're wrong

At my computer I meditate on the afar
My body is not dressed up and lit
But I care too little to talk to fools
Though often I hole up at home all day
I am the very soul of my room

All they see is a Geeky Girl
and not the numberless rooms in my eyes
where they are arrested, imprisoned
and only when they know who I am
will I unlock their cells

But now they see me on the news
on their computer screens, suddenly
they become my friends and family

Translated by Jonathan Chiang

宅女的房間

他們說 我盯著螢幕的眼神呆若木雞
他們說 我瘦瘦的身軀柴柴的
他們說 我說話期期艾艾
他們說 我的名字叫宅女

他們都錯了

我電腦前的沉思　有一個遠方
我的身體　只是還沒打扮 還沒被點燃
還有　我懶得跟笨蛋講話
我雖然常常窩在家
但我是我房間的靈魂

宅女是他們所見
他們不知道我眼裡有無限個房間
反將他們一一拘提　監禁
他們必須知道我是誰之後
我才會打開鎖　放他們走

現在 他們都在新聞裡
電腦螢幕前
看到我了
他們都是我的親友了

Yen Ai-Lin (颜艾琳)

Super Vending Machine

I am thirsty.

I put in all my money.
Nothing comes out.

So I give it my arms and legs
and stick my head in
but not enough.

I let it swallow the rest of me.
It sits there.

Finally, I insert my soul.
It spits out a skeleton
and displays: *Sorry, no change*

Translated by Jonathan Chiang

超级贩卖机

我觉得饥渴。

我投下所有的钱，
它什么也没给我。

我只好把手脚给它
又将头递过去
但还不够。

我继续让它吞噬其它的肢体，
它仍旧不给我任何东西。

最后我把灵魂也投给了它。
它吐出一副骸骨
并漠然显示
「恕不找零」

Yen Ai-Lin (颜艾琳)

Winter Beyond Clouds, Within Rain

Why do today's clouds cry
before wandering?
A lonely little brother
crosses the street with a huge umbrella
to fetch his sister from daycare.
I come out for a decent cup of coffee,
only to miss the man who sneaks out of work for our affair.
Turtledoves, hidden in an umbrella tree,
watch the kindergarteners playing hide-and-seek.
This world is so lonely
and so fickle —
(An unemployed father
sells his soft body to the god of death just now.
Four hours later,
the child will play hide-and-seek with his father forever.)
A bit of excitement —
will make bored citizens willing to live on.
A bit of possession —
an empty life addicted to desire.
A map —
of derailed affairs.
But a cloud knows,
not defined by such
quotidian details.
She is just a description.
(One day, the rain picks on the little sister.)
Contrasted.
(I missed the most passionate affair of my life, that day, black clouds)
Outcasted.
(Dad is hiding in the clouds)
Other than rain…
(a city of poets are downing Prozac)

(May I ask, who reads poems on a rainy day?)
A jobless cloud;
I want to console it by a winter sea.

Translated by Jonathan Chiang

雲之外，雨之內的冬天

今天的雲在準備流浪之前，
為何哭了？
孤單的小弟弟
撐著一支巨大的雨傘過街，
要去接安親班的妹妹。
我出來找一杯好喝的咖啡，
卻錯過翹班的他找我偷情。
斑鳩躲在欖仁樹上，
看幼稚園中班的小孩玩抓迷藏。
這世界如此寂寞，
又如此無常，
（剛剛一個失業的父親，
將自己很輕的肉體拍賣給死神。
四個小時之後，
那個小孩將永遠與父親玩著躲貓貓。）
一些些熱鬧，
就讓無聊的人們願意活下去。
一些些佔有欲，
就讓虛無的人生有了慾望的癮。
一張地圖，
就產生出軌的綺想。
但是，雲知道
它不在這些日常裡，
被定位。
它只是被描述。
（某天，小妹妹被雨欺負）
被陪襯。
（我錯過一生中最激情的外遇，那天，烏雲）
被置外。
（爸爸就躲在雲的裡面）
除了下雨之外...
（整城的詩人都在吞百憂解）

（請問，有誰在雨天讀詩？）
被開除的雲，
我要去冬天的海邊安慰它。

Hole

A hole appeared in the bedroom.
Eyes just woke up,
thought it was a dream that had not ended.
A full-stop in waiting
never appeared.
Instead the hole got bigger,
darker.
Like a cyclone it engulfed me,
that abyss, as if
I fell into a woman's birth canal.

Like a copper coin,
I was thrown in
and spit out.
In the largest and loneliest vending machine in the universe,
I found my life exposed and on sale.
Playing games, gods
used wounded weary hearts
to convert my story.

No, all these are mine, mine,
no one can take them away!
I opened my mouth and yelled, but the hole jumped into my mouth.
Gradually
my fingers, limbs, body, five senses…
shrouded by a black hole.

Now I am a hole.
A shameless, inhumane emptiness:
it hangs in its universe,
completely sealed,
and vanishes.

Translated by Jonathan Chiang

洞

卧室出现一个洞。
刚睡醒的眼睛，
以为是梦　未结束。
等待中的句点
一直未出现，
洞反而越来越大、
越来越深黑。
它忽然飓风似地将我卷入，
那无底的深邃，彷佛
我掉进了妇女分娩的产道。

我如一枚铜板，
被投入
又被吐出，
在宇宙最大的寂寞贩卖机里；
我发现我的人生被公开展售。
众神以游戏的心态
用一颗颗伤痕累累的心，
来兑换我的故事。

「不，这都是我的，我的，
谁也不准拿走！」
我张嘴大喊，洞却跳进我的嘴里。
逐渐地
我的手指、四肢、躯体、五官…….
被黑洞重重地涂染。

现在，我是一个洞了。
一个没有羞耻、没有人性的兀物 ；
悬于自身的宇宙，
完全地封锁，
而且
消失了。

Yu Bang (育邦)

You May Be Called China

You are in the window
I look into the depths of Time

We meet
We do not know it

Your hands sweat a little
I am writing a letter

You float like a corpse on a vast lake
You have a Chinese smile
I turn to hide in the woods and climb up the hill

You discard the afterglow
The gathering dusk is my home

You're gone, there's no place you're not
I vow to elude gravity

I have heard
You may be called China, or you may not

Translated by Li Yiliang

你也许叫中国

你在窗口
我在时光的深处眺望

我们相遇
我们并不知晓

你的手微微出汗
我在写信

你漂浮在广袤的湖面上，死尸一般
你的笑容很中国
我转过头，隐身到密林处，向山上攀登

你摒弃余辉
暮色是我的家园

你湮灭了，你无处不在
摆脱重力成为我矢志不渝的游戏

如是我闻
你也许叫中国，或者不是

Mi-lou

—To Zang Bei

Torrential rainstorm, this world the sea
Mi-lou becomes a temple[15]
The Buddha has been teaching us
Forgetting is the best practice

A desire-believer
under the weight of history
routed on the axis of morality
leaving behind Wild Chinese Viburnum, riddles
and a succession of non-deterministic kingdoms
a betrayal of body and distance
as if we had never been young

Shugang solemn[16]
a small boat on the earth
transporting to us
withered flowers and compassion

Death and dust
cling to pure rhetoric—
Mi-lou is no longer Mi-lou
Mi-lou is still Mi-lou

Translated by Li Yiliang

---

[15] Mi-lou originally refers to a labyrinth-like palace built by emperor Yang of the Sui Dynasty in Yangzhou at the beginning of the 7th century for his indulgent enjoyment. Now the relic is still to be seen in the northwestern suburb of Yangzhou City.

[16] Shugang, located in the northwestern suburb of Yangzhou City, where Mi-lou was originally built. Now it is a park, about two kilometers northwest of Fucheng (Yangzhou), across the Yangtze River in Jinling (now Nanjing).

迷楼

——给臧北

暴雨如注，尘世如海
迷楼幻化为寺庙
佛陀谆谆教导我们
遗忘是最好的修行

欲望信仰者
在繁缛的历史限制下
溃败于道德之轴
留下了琼花、谜语和一连串非确定性王国
背叛肉体与远方
仿佛我们从来都不曾年轻过

蜀冈静穆
如大地上的一叶扁舟
向我们运送
凋零的鲜花和最后的怜悯

死亡与尘埃
固守着纯粹修辞——
迷楼不是迷楼
迷楼还是迷楼

Yu Bang (育邦)

Middle-age

I know that
I made love to the world
defiling my days and past versions of me
I am no longer myself
I bring back a leaf a thousand miles away
When I see a pigeon, I am moved to tears
In the human forest
I always pick those colorful
strange mushrooms
because they are poisonous
In the temple crowded with Bodhisattvas
every stick of incense I light so lonely
fades with melancholy and annoyance
I hang up the sword in the empty sky
because it's tired
I rub my hands in vain
greet the ageing sun
simple as a drop of water
it withers away
silence within it

Translated by Li Yiliang

中年

我知道
我与世界的媾和
玷污了我的日子以及从前的我
我有别于我自己
我从千里之外带回一片树叶
当我看到鸽子，就会流泪
在人与人构成的森林里
我总是采撷那些
色彩绚烂、光怪陆离的蘑菇
仅仅因为它们是有毒的
在菩萨众多的大庙里
我所点燃的每一柱香都那么孤单
忧郁而烦躁地明灭
我把剑挂在虚无的天空中
因为它已疲惫
我徒劳地搓一搓手
迎接日趋衰老的夕阳
它简朴得如一滴清水
凋零，流逝
却拥有寂静

Yu Bang (育邦)

Returning Home

Carrying the wooden sword
from the other side of the world
I took a boat back
Chezhou River filled with my time
beyond the sea
near the village where the stars reside
is my hometown

I came ashore at Grain Depot Wharf
I had unlimited time

There was a path under the papaya tree
That's the poet's secret way
Then the papaya trees were cut down
The path hung in the night sky
The cuckoo's cries reverberated through the grove
like ancient relics

Wind, snow, roses with blood
wiped my sorrow
Oh, the heart of a child
glows in the dust
The river sobs and in full voice
the sea roars
the names of the drowned children
They are all my friends

Translated by Li Yiliang

返乡

我背负木剑
从世界的另一边
乘船归来
车轴河里落满了我的光阴
在海的那边
靠近星辰居住的小镇
是我的故乡

我从粮站码头上岸
我拥有无限的时间

木瓜树下有一条小路
那是诗人的秘密小道
后来，木瓜树被砍伐了
它只能悬挂在夜空中
杜鹃的啼鸣依旧回荡在小树林中
已成为古老的遗迹

风，雪，带血的玫瑰
为我拂拭忧伤
哦，那颗小时候的心
在灰尘中发光
河流呜咽，大海咆哮
突然大声说出
那些被淹死孩子的名字
——他们都是我的朋友

Yu Bang (育邦)

Kid in the Neighboring Seat

The oasis created by the anesthetic is endless
The evil flowers bloom on the ruins
We held filthy water in our hands
consecrating the snow
Breeding Death
we devoured the darkness
We threw ourselves into thc long night
Our eternal cause

Oh, the kid sitting next to me overheard the formula
how adults make playdough
If I die
please transfer the power of Death to him
Crown him
in the rising snowstorm

The world
generously gives him seven days

Translated by Li Yiliang

邻座的孩子

麻醉剂开辟的绿洲无边无际
废墟上开满了邪恶的花朵
我们手捧污秽的水
供奉着雪
我们吞食黑暗
饲养着死亡
投身于漫漫长夜
这永恒的事业

哦，邻座的孩子偷听到大人们制作橡皮泥的配方
如果我死了
请把死亡的权柄转移到他的手中
在飞升的风雪中
为他加冕

世界也会慷慨地
给他七天时间

Zang Di (臧棣)

After the New Society for Wisdom

—in memory of Seamus Heaney 1939-2013

The love of Ireland. Far enough
but not unfamiliar. With every dig,
Ireland's orchids follow
that new wisdom, and find in the language of loneliness
a supreme support. The deep green tips of leaves sway
the careful heart. How will the pistils trembling
in those worded intentions regard
this side of human life, now poetry's prisoners.
As for the hole left by the digging, only sweat
can fill it. Only this kind of hole
leads to a deeper trust in this wearisome world.
Call the after-images—
they've already persisted this long
in a landscape set in the landscape. Love is ice.
If you don't believe it, you can go see for yourself.
The last day of August came like an elephant.
Don't look at me that way—for now, I'm blind.
Blind men for dark times.
As Delmore Schwartz, Humboldt's model
in *Humboldt's Gift*, painfully said—
"For like a gun is touch." All grim,
but still you open the blacksmith's oily shop curtain,
to teach me to be like a hammer, to trust in every touch.

Translated by Eleanor Goodman

随着那新鲜的深度协会
—纪念谢默斯·希尼 (Seamus Heaney 1939-2013)

爱尔兰的爱。足够遥远
但绝不陌生。每一次挖掘，
爱尔兰的兰，都会随着
那新鲜的深度，在孤独的语言中
找到美妙的支撑。深绿的叶尖摇动
一个细心。动摇的花蕊
在这样的口风中，会如何看待
人生的片面，已成为诗的俘虏呢。
至于挖掘留下的坑，只有汗水
才能填满。也只有这样的坑，
才能在时世的艰难中加深一次信任。
给倒影打一个电话吧——
既然它们已在风景中的风景里
坚持了这么久。爱是冰。
不信的话，你可以自己动手试一试。
八月的最后一天，像一头大象。
别这么看着我。我现在是个盲人。
这样的底线，就该有这样的盲人。
德尔默·施瓦茨，即“洪堡的礼物”中
洪堡的原型，他悲伤地说过——
“接触是一杆枪”。情况的确很严峻，
但是你，坚持掀开油腻的铁匠铺门帘，
教会我像铁锤一样，去信任每一次触摸。

Zang Di (臧棣)

Golden Secret Series

When I lower my head, I see only these chrysanthemums,
golden guides, the little hands curve up and out, like the cirrus of mollusks.
Only with a careless glance do they become bright yellow petals.

And right now, I am as careful as a broken string.
Raised this well, they surely understand politics,
and so, something profound about the universe is there in the politeness of plants.

When I lift my head, I glimpse the person who waters them.
She isn't a gardener, but it seems she has an even better method,
and knows exactly how to sprinkle water on the key spots.

Relatively speaking, there are countless secrets behind every person.
But her secrets aren't behind her, they're between me and the chrysanthemums,
that's right, her secrets will always be in front of her.

Translated by Eleanor Goodman

金色的秘密丛书

低头时，我只看见这菊花，
金色向导，小小的手臂曲张着，像软体动物的触须。
粗心看，才貌合成艳黄的花瓣。

而我现在，心细得就像一根断弦。
养得这么好，一定懂政治，
于是，植物的礼貌就有了宇宙的深意。

一抬头，我瞥见了给它浇水的人。
她不是园丁，不过看起来她有更好的方法，
知道如何把水浇到点子上。

稍一比较，多数人的背后都有无数的秘密。
而她的秘密不在她身后，在我和菊花之间，
没错，她的秘密永远在她的前面。

Zang Di (臧棣)

Delight in Creation Series

In between us is a bird.
As soon as you open your eyes, he flies away.
He helps us gradually adapt to our optimal distance.
He tucks all of perception into a pair of wings.

When he flies toward you, only a centimeter of time remains.
The first time I wanted to catch hold of myself.
I wanted to seize that wing-carried self before your eyes.
For the first time I felt a wonderful thing hadn't betrayed the truth.

Between me and the two of us there is some thing
that flies faster than a bird. Before our eyes I wanted
to relax into a new role. Its whole weight together
wouldn't be more than a bird. It has a beautiful head,

you can borrow it anytime. It has a long tail,
and you might as well use the nerves with which they hold up the universe.
You're amazed that on that tiny bird body
all of life is reflected.

Translated by Eleanor Goodman

原创性愉悦丛书

在我们之间有一只鸟。
只要你一睁眼，它就在飞。
它让我们渐渐适应了我们之间的最佳距离。
它给所有的感觉都插上了一对翅膀。

当它飞向你时，时间只剩下一厘米。
我第一次想捉住我自己。
我想在你面前，捕捉到一个带翅膀的我。
我第一次感觉到奇妙从未背叛过真理。

在我和你我之间有一种东西
飞得比鸟还快。我想在你我面前
松开一个全新的角色。它所有的重量加起来
也不会超过一只鸟。它有漂亮的头，

你随时可以借来一用。它有长长的尾巴，
你不妨用它们来翘一翘宇宙的神经。
你奇怪，这么小的一只鸟身上，
竟然有全部的生活的影子。

Zang Di (臧棣)

Night Bird Series

I dreamt each time we're together, three people are there.
You said, the other one is a bird.

When I call your name, the bird calls as well.
When you call my name, he's still calling.

His voice is like a pipe collecting night dew,
stretching out from the dark window.

When we're quiet, his calls continue.
The calls imply something, but don't name names.

His calls contain another vaster cry,
a kind I thought couldn't exist outside of human screams.

Translated by Eleanor Goodman

夜鸟丛书

我梦见，我们在一起时一直是三个人。
你说，那另外一个其实是只鸟。

我叫你的名字时，那只鸟也一直叫。
你叫我的名字时，它仍在叫。

它的叫声，像一根缀着夜露的管子，
从黝黑的窗外伸了进来。

我们安静下来时，它的叫声依然持续不断。
它的叫声有确定的含义，只是里面没有一个名字。

它的叫声里包含着一种更大的呼唤——
以前，我以为那样的声音绝不可能存在于人的叫喊之外。

Zang Di (臧棣)

In Hualien Series

A small place has large smells—aside from the smell of Wenzhou wontons
there is the smell of wax apples, aside from the smell of wild narcissus
there is the smell of the ocean, aside from the sugar-apple cakes
there is the smell of eel, and aside from the fact that the air is very fresh
there is another indescribable natural freshness. The conclusion I came to
is a man can live conflicted with life, but shouldn't
be conflicted with the lifecycle of flowers. People's trees
give people's flowers a hard time, but this has never been

a good reason for anything. Waking up in the morning,
the sun is like a golden hook, catching the fish of our bodies.
Not getting hooked is just luck; and not being hooked is good fun.
But fun at best just demonstrates the baseline isn't complex.
It's obvious that here the ocean means two things—
the thundering waves are like a blue flatiron, trying to smooth down our
experiences.
But the ocean inside our bodies, its purity suddenly heightened,
tosses our personality up onto the wharf of an iris flower.

The vision of outsiders is only a projection,
the more they project, the less they'll be cheated.
Speaking of emotions, inside fate, whose bizarreness is from instinct,
is a you who explains the profound simply. As for returning home,
life that has a talent for ordinariness is important, but it certainly isn't
as important as you think it is. On local screens,
there are only cerulean customs that maintain their connections.
Every instant, the self is inexhaustible.

To recover into absolute silence means one hasn't seen clearly.
Due to this, I thought, a real recovery should be
a theme configured to directly address men's secrets.
Saying that, it would be better if the scenery seemed a bit finite.
The local scenery takes the truth of time and relegates it
to one side of the Pacific Ocean. Pointing with any finger,
blue sky is bigger than daylight. Whatever secrets I can discover are surely
in Hualien, where the days are large and the nights are small.

Translated by Eleanor Goodman

人在花莲丛书

小地方有大味道，除了温州馄饨的味道
还有莲雾的味道，除了野水仙的味道
还有大海的味道，除了释迦麻薯饼的味道
还有鳗鱼的味道，除了空气很新鲜
还有说不出的自然的新鲜。我得出的结论是
人尽可以矛盾于生活，但不该
矛盾于花开花落。人之花
艰难于人之树，但这从来就不是

一个很好的理由。早上醒来，
太阳像一个金钩子，钓我们身上的鱼。
没上钩，是运气；不上钩，是真的很好玩。
但好玩，顶多是表明底线不复杂。
很明显，大海在此有两个意思——
轰鸣的巨浪像蓝熨斗，试图将我们的经验抚平。
而我们身体里的大海，纯度突然增高，
将我们的个性掀翻在鸢尾花的码头。

外地人的眼光只是一种投影，
投射得越多，受骗的机会就会越小。
讲感情，命运吊诡于本能里
有一个深入浅出的你。论归宿，
人生大可平凡于天赋很重要，但绝对没有
你想象得那么重要。本地的屏幕上，
只有蔚蓝的风俗始终保持连贯。
每一秒钟，自我都取之不尽。

恢复到天机不可泄露，还是没见底。
我由此想到，真正的恢复，应该是
专门针对男人的秘密而设置的一个主题。
说起来，风光似乎有限一点会更好。
本地的风光将时间的真理淘汰在
太平洋的边上。用手随便一指，
蓝天就比白天大。我能发现的秘密确乎是
在花莲，白天很大，夜晚很小。

Zang Di (臧棣)

Maple Syrup Primer

That whole afternoon, the local maple syrup
wriggles its amber figure
and from all sorts of unfamiliar angles
it hawks its wares to you with sweet ancient fists;

To fight back, must you really
cover your eyes with the politics
of time again? The target is ready-made,
it has been hidden in your body all along;

When it becomes a clear target, it offers
a match of wits, even prettier than objectivity.
All that must be explained is: here,
ancient has its own connotations.

From shiny to sticky, it doesn't hide
that the sap was collected from maples
forty meters tall; as for those little holes drilled into trunks
as paths for sweetness, their history

goes back sixteen hundred years. This alone
shows the shortcomings of your memory,
only by pouring this syrup
can one return to the wild—

and there, with primeval absorption,
the violence of the sweetness practices
a perfect restraint, and it is able, from the inside,
to awaken you to your pure original form.

Translated by Eleanor Goodman

枫糖液入门

整个下午，本地的枫糖液
扭动着琥珀色的腰肢，
从各种陌生的角度，
向你兜售一击甜蜜的老拳；

如何出手，难道还需要
用时间的政治把你的眼睛
再蒙上一次吗？靶子是现成的，
一直都隐藏在你身上；

即便明确成对象，也是彼此
较着劲，比客观还漂亮。
唯一需要解释的是，这里，
老，究竟涉及怎样的含义。

剔透到浓稠，但它并没隐瞒
这树蜜是从高达四十米的枫树上
采集来的；而那些开凿在树干的小洞，
作为甜蜜的通道，它们的历史

已有一千六百年。仅凭这一点，
它已指出，你的记忆存有怎样的缺陷，
且亟待通过这些蜜液的注入，
才能重返荒野中的停留——

那里，经过原始的消化，
甜蜜的暴力仿佛已练就了
一种绝对的分寸，足以从内部
将你直接唤醒到纯粹的原型之中。

Zang Di (臧棣)

Spinach

This beautiful spinach hasn't once
hidden you in its green shirt.
You've never worn
any kind of green shirt.
You avoid this kind of imagery–
yet I can clearly remember
how your silent flesh resembled
a seed at its extreme.
Why does spinach look
beautiful? How
do I know you will wonder,
but won't ask the question?
Washing the spinach, I feel
its deep greenness
like a child born of the plant and me.
So spinach answers the question
of how we can see in our lives
angels others say don't exist.
The beauty of spinach is fragile–
when we face the mere fifty square meters
of standard living space, this vivid spinach
is the most fragile politics. On the surface
a bit wild, difficult to clean–
its beauty one might say
is sustained by the power of little irritations.
Yet its nutrition determines
its value, not to the left or the right.

Translated by Eleanor Goodman

菠菜

美丽的菠菜不曾把你
藏在它们的绿衬衣里。
你甚至没有穿过
任何一种绿颜色的衬衣，
你回避了这样的形象；
而我能更清楚地记得
你沉默的肉体就像
一粒极端的种子。
为什么菠菜看起来
是美丽的？为什么
我知道你会想到
但不会提出这样的问题？
我冲洗菠菜时感到
它们碧绿的质量摸上去
就像是我和植物的孩子。
如此，菠菜回答了
我们怎样才能在我们的生活中
看见对他们来说
似乎并不存在的天使的问题。
菠菜的美丽是脆弱的
当我们面对一个只有五十平方米的
标准的空间时，鲜明的菠菜
是最脆弱的政治。表面上，
它们有些零乱，不易清理；
它们的美丽也可以说
是由繁琐的力量来维持的；
而它们的营养纠正了
它们的价格，不左也不右。

Zhai Yongming (翟永明)

Marches in the Second World

I've seen marches in the Second World
I've flown by them on my bike
People were walking slowly
leading dogs holding cats
and pushing babies in strollers

On march days the weather
is always great Large white clouds—
abundant with nature's gifts—
always float in the sky above the troops
becoming their cotton flags
Their moderately paced footsteps
seem to be treading on cotton
falling behind not from exhaustion

These beautiful marches that take place every few days
are just like this country: one hundred percent
pure juice and natural flavor filling the streets
with majestic flowers in bloom

I've experienced another march once
This time it looked like blood was splattering
There were bricks stones and shields
There was a bust of Che Guevara
There were rebellious youths running
and police officers in pursuit
This time I fell behind them

Lovers gasped for air as they fled
and sang guerilla love songs
Other people crowded around from all sides and directions
then dispersed Water flowed down
It wasn't really high-pressure water
Rather, an arced stream, cold enough
to wash away the rage on their faces

第二世界的游行

我看过第二世界的游行
我骑车从他们前面飞过
他们走得很慢
牵着狗 抱着猫
推着小Baby……

游行的日子 天气
总是很好 那些得天独厚的
云朵 又大又白
总是飘在队伍上空
成为他们的棉花旗帜
他们不疾不缓的脚步
也象踩在棉花上
不是因力竭而落下

这些隔三岔五的美丽的游行
就象这个国家 百分之百
原汁原味地 绽放着
满城满街 大气磅礴的花

别的游行我还经历过一次
这次看上去血光飞溅
有砖头 石块和透明盾牌
有切.格瓦纳的头像
有暴动的年轻人在跑
警察在追
这次我掉在了他们的后面

恋人们在逃跑时喘息
和唱着他们的游击队情歌
其余的人从四面八方围拢
又散开 水落下来了
不是动真格的高压水
而是弧线的，寒冷的也足以
洗去他们脸上的狂怒

Zhai Yongming (翟永明))

The cockscomb red gushing
out from their strange hair
wasn't a brutal red
nor was it the red of an injury
It most resembled a pure color
seen in violent games

next day when I walked by
the town square again   I discovered
the garbage cans and bus stops
knocked over by the dark night
had already been lifted up again In the sunlight
these city government installations
were even more robust than the private shops lining the streets

Translated by Jami Proctor Xu

他们奇怪的头发上
喷出鸡冠式的红
不是惨烈的红色
也不是伤痛的红色
而是最接近暴力游戏的
一种纯净的颜色

第二天　我再次走过
这个广场 发现
被黑夜推倒的垃圾桶
和巴士停靠站
已被举起 在阳光下
这些市政设施
比沿街的私人小店铺更硬朗

Zhai Yongming (翟永明)

White Corridor

I've seen a tiny white passage
Wavering on sleepless nights
A gusty wind that rustles and wrinkles my skirts
Little drops of blood are flowering
Like the humdrum existence   of so many signatures

I've seen a sick girl pale as jade draped across the bed
Turning her beautiful face from side to side
The reasons for her fever have broken up the summer heat
I run past a vanished door
Where a half-opened chest cavity
Has transformed an arrogant heart
Into vital hopes

I've seen a lonely little corridor
A woman in a white coat walks quietly in
The sound of her weeping travels
Mother's two blood-covered hands appear and then vanish
Spinning in my eyes
Burdening me with the afternoon
The brilliance of the scalpel
The tightly stitched rays of light

I've seen my mother's narrow passage
Awakened into darkness with a start
A life-force like water tugged me gently
This is a kind of forcible escape
An immaculate little passage
The way it's rent apart   and I'm pulled out
The sick body contains a botanical garden you might see in a dream
A plethora of diseases have come to lodge there
Without origin or outcome
Without fatigue
Wide eyes stare at the rips in white clothing
So full of allure
Summer's invalid girl feels her way forward
Mild mannered   snow-white sidelong stares
That dream of sweeping everything clean

Translated by Andrea Lingenfelter

白色的走廊

我见过白色的小小走廊
在不眠之夜移动
衣裙吹皱沙沙作响的风
小小的血滴开着花
象很多签名 单单调调的存在

我见过玉体横陈的病女孩
把美貌的头转动
她高烧的理由把夏天的温度破坏
我跑过失踪的门
那儿半开半闭的胸膛
把内心的嚣张变成
一些活生生的愿望

我见过孤独的小小走廊
穿白罩衫的女人悄悄走来
她哭泣的声音传得远
母亲沾满血迹的两手忽隐忽现
在我眼中逡巡
让我担负起一个下午
手术刀的光芒
以及密密缝合的光线

我见过母亲的小小走廊
在黑暗中惊醒
似水的生命力把我轻轻托起
这是被迫出逃的方式
这是纯洁的小小走廊
分裂的方式 拖着我
病体有如梦中的百草园
栖息着多种多样的疫疾
没有来龙去脉
没有困倦
眼睁睁看着白衣的裂纹
充满魔力
夏天的病女孩摸索着走来
温顺的 雪白的凝睇
带着扫荡一切的幻觉

Zhai Yongming (翟永明)

"Lightly Injured People, Gravely Wounded City"

Here they come, the lightly injured
Their gauze as white as their faces
Their wounds sewn up more neatly than the war
Here they come, the lightly injured
Carrying what they cherish
The parts that have not died
They strip off their uniforms   they wash themselves clean
Use checks and credit cards

The gravely wounded city seethes with energy
Its pulse and temperature rising and falling
Faster than war
Slower than fear
Casts off its bandages and artificial legs
It has bled a green secretion
And provided the indomitable power of stone
One of the lightly injured   raises his head to look
At those esthetic edifices

Six thousand bombs come pounding down
Leaving an arms depot in flames
Six thousand blast sites
Like six thousand gravely wounded eyes
In a rush they light up faces
Of thousands of women who have husbands
Men who have wives   unmarried men and women
Bodies covered in sulphur   or asphalt
At their feet, twisted metal

The lightly injured   now set out
Heavily wounded maps in hand
They split up to search
For the new vessels of tall buildings
Forms thin and light and pointed
The brain of this city
Extends its spikes

轻伤的人，重伤的城市

轻伤的人过来了
他们的白色纱布象他们的脸
他们的伤痕比战争缝合得好
轻伤的人过来了
担着心爱的东西
没有断气的部份
脱掉军服 洗净全身
使用支票和信用卡

一个重伤的城市血气翻涌
脉搏和体温在起落
比战争快
比恐惧慢
重伤的城市
扔掉了假腿和绷带
现在它已流出绿色分泌物
它已提供石材的万能之能
一个轻伤的人 仰头
看那些美学上的建筑

六千颗炸弹砸下来
留下一个燃烧的军械所
六千颗弹着点
象六千只重伤之眼
匆忙地映照出
那几千个有夫之妇
有妇之夫 和未婚男女的脸庞
他们的身上全是硫磺，或者沥青
他们的脚下是拆掉的钢架

轻伤的人 从此
拿着一本重伤的地图
他们分头去寻找那些
新的器皿大楼
薄形，轻形和尖形
这个城市的脑袋
如今尖锐锋利的伸出去

So easy to chop off
Yet frightening off a number of cuts

2000, Berlin

Translated by Andrea Lingenfelter

既容易被砍掉
也吓退了好些伤口

2000 年于柏林

Zhang Zhihao (张执浩)

Diary, Or Stars in the Wee Hours

It hasn't been like this for long—
I lay my right hand on your left breast
But you sleep more soundly
How long should I keep my hand there in the dark
To be touched by the shape it ought to have
I am touched by myself in the dark
As the stars in the wee hours twinkle by themselves

Translated by Zhang Dongying

日记，或后半夜的星空

已经很久没有这样过了——
我的右手不经意间搭在了你的左乳上
你反而睡得更香
而我要在黑暗中将这个姿势保持多久
才能为这只手重新回忆起了它应有的形状而感动
我在黑暗中自我感动着
就像后半夜的星空独自闪烁

Zhang Zhihao (张执浩)

Non Fiction

Taking a pickled pork knuckle to the wet market
I asked the hottest lady butcher to chop it into cubes
And bought a piece of tofu and a bunch of garlic chives
Halfway home it drizzled
Parents with schoolbags on their backs
Little kids dawdling on their way home:
I'm not holding your hand to cross the street
Passing by the academy, I lowered my head
And glimpsed myself
carrying plastic bags in four colors
in crowds of five and six colors
which were merely levees burst by the floods

Translated by Zhang Dongying

纪实

拎一只腊猪蹄去菜市
请最好看的肉案女剁成块状
买一块豆腐一把韭菜回来
毛毛雨在中途落下
背书包的父母
磨蹭着不肯回家的小人儿
是否不过马路就能我行我素
路过读书院的时候我低头
看了一眼自己，我看见我
拎着四种颜色的塑料袋
走在五颜六色的人群中
而人群不过是不断溃堤的防波堤

Zhang Zhihao (张执浩)

Sentimental Streetscape

The last thing I can bear to see is
a young girl on a bench
tearfully facing the person on the other end of the line
Drizzle covers the tips of her hair
Gingko leaves cling to the back and foot of the bench
The last thing I can bear to hear is
a maiden's hopeless begging
which is for promise rather than
the person far away at the other end
Drizzle drops indifferently
Heavy Traffic flows slowly
Unable to cross the street
I stand on the roadside, getting wet
enduring the life I'm least willing to live.

Translated by Liu Qianqian

伤感的街景

我最不忍心看到的是
少女坐在街边的长椅上
满面泪水地面对着电话那头的人
毛毛雨落满了她的发梢
银杏树的叶子紧贴着椅背椅脚
我最不忍心听见的是
少女无望的哀求——
那是对承诺的哀求而不是
对那个远在空气另一端的人
毛毛雨无关痛痒地落下
车流缓慢而紧凑
我过不了大街
湿漉漉地站在马路边
经受着我最不愿意经历的生活

Zhang Zhihao (张执浩)

Spring Thunder No. 3

Men were queuing in front of the urinal
Taking turns to pee
Finally, it came to me
This little kid crowded my back
Even stretched his head to my front
Which turned off my tap abruptly
Of course I didn't want to stop
We were at a rest stop
Eyes squinting, my mind fled to an open field
Where the little kid was pissing into the wind
With wide eyes fixed on
The dark clouds whirling
The tempest was coming
Finally, it was my turn to contribute a shower
Quiet was the washroom, there
Only I heard the thunder

Translated by Chen Hongbo

春雷3号

男人们排队站在小便器前
轮流着小便
终于轮到我了
一个小孩在我身后催促
他甚至把脑袋伸到了我的前面
我的尿意戛然而止
但我并不想放弃
这是在高速公路的休息区
我眯上眼睛想象着原野上
迎风而尿的少年
睁大眼睛望着
正在天上翻卷的乌云
暴雨将至
终于轮到我献上甘霖
安静的洗手间内
隐忍的雷声只有我一个人听见了

Zhang Zhihao (张执浩)

Where Did You Pour Out The Rice Water?

Busy as I am in the kitchen,
My mother-in-law is busier.
Whatever I throw down, she picks up.
On the cutting board I shred sweet peppers and ginger,
at the sink she is washing cups and plates.
The more cups and plates washed,
the more dish towels appear.
I wish she would bask in the sun,
with my father-in-law on the balcony
watering orchids and aloes.
Spring is here, grey swallows fly around the eaves,
Azaleas are blooming while withering.
I yearn for solitude in the kitchen
I am ready to cook,
but want everyone seated at the table
when I turn off the stove.
The hot oil in the pot is hissing,
The tap is still running,
My mother-in-law cannot help whispering:
"Where did you pour out the rice water?"

Translated by Zhang Qin

你把淘米水倒哪儿去了

我在厨房里忙碌的时候
我的岳母也在我身边忙碌着
我丢什么，她就捡什么
我在砧板上切彩椒和姜丝
她在盥洗池边擦洗杯盘
越洗杯盘越多
抹布也越来越多
我希望她出去晒太阳
我的岳父正在阳台上
给几盆兰草、芦荟浇水
春天来了，灰背鸟绕着屋檐飞
杜鹃花边开边落
我希望在我开始炒菜的时候
厨房里只有我一个人
而当我关掉炉火的时候
餐桌旁已经各就各位
油锅已经滋滋作响了
水龙头仍然在滴水
我的岳母还在那里嘀咕：
“你把淘米水倒哪儿去了？”

Zhang Zhihao (张执浩)

In the Gathering Dusk

My father walks up and down in the dusk.
He's always the last person to walk in the door.
I can hardly recognize him except for his back.
He stoops slightly, rises early
and sits under the eaves waiting for darkness.
I can hardly recognize him.
Sometimes I pull up a bench and sit opposite him,
looking at him as if he was
a child smiling with wry amusement.
Rough hands on his knees
as if pushed into the photo studio,
so wronged, so embarrassed.

Translated by Li Yiliang

暮色中

我父亲在暮色中走来走去
他总是最后一个走进家门的人
除了背影，我几乎认不出他
当他日益佝偻，一大早
就坐在屋檐下等候天黑
我更加认不出他了
有时我也拉一张板凳在他对面坐下
仔细看他像一个孩子
讪笑着
粗糙的手掌搭在膝盖上
仿佛被人推进了照相馆
有些委屈，不好意思

Zhang Zhihao (张执浩)

Someone Who Talked to a Baby

The woman talking to the baby has her back to me,
she sat on a bench in the small garden.
I thought she was murmuring to herself.
When I got closer, I saw a baby girl in her arms.
It was a clear day after rain.
The fresh leaves shivered in the soft breeze.
The world I love has shrunk.
Now it reduces to a cuddle.
I am looking wistfully at her arms.
I am in her arms, babbling.

Translated by Li Yiliang

和婴儿说话的人

和婴儿说话的人背对我
坐在小花园的条凳上
我以为她在自言自语
走近了才看见她怀抱里的女婴
这是雨后清明的一天
新鲜的树叶在微风中颤栗
我所热爱的世界已经很小了
现在缩成了一个怀抱
我在怀抱外无限眷念地望着
我在怀抱里“呀呀咿咿”

Zhao Si (赵四)

Green Love

Riding on a bicycle, singing in the rain all along her way,
a dark-green raincoat she ran into
popping out of it half of a pure face of an ephebe,
a flower half-open right before her eyes.

A nightmare fallen out of pupils,
cold-blooded intuition of reptiles.

Many web-footed umbrellas,
spiders of colors, crawl in the streets and lanes,
as an earthworm stretches in the rain, longer and longer until it breaks in two,
then brains headed in opposite directions.

Dancing out of their sky, they are too human.

In the overwhelming posture
of pouring a glass of water,
wet trees pin over the street,
in an arching green fog.

Translated by Xuan Yuan & Tim Lilburn

绿 爱

在雨中骑着自行车一路高歌
突然撞上一领墨绿色雨衣里
半张纯粹的人脸
宛如花开

瞳孔中跌出噩梦
爬虫的冰冷直觉

一只只长了蹼的雨伞
五色的蜘蛛在街巷里爬
一条蚯蚓在雨水中把自己越拖越长
断成两节
然后两个脑袋背道而驰

人性的，太人性的舞蹈

一杯水的丰姿
在倾倒
湿了的整条街树
拱立绿雾

Zhao Si (赵四)

Emptying

In a gust of autumn wind, a small car
chugging hard, all leaves of the tree chug along
to the rhythm of exodus & return. A row of green turtles
rolls onto their yellow bellies and floats down the street;
wearing a fox mask, perching on a tree,
sitting on a river bank, autumn howls and watches;
stars managing traffic lights quit work early
on Thanksgiving afternoon; waves of cars
chugging and stalling. The fox hangs its sighs
on leaves flying back home; crunchiness and bitterness
are the taste of west wind; the arrival of bitterness unleashes
fierce autumn gusts; splendour surpassing all,
a grand occasion, the aphasic master takes a resplendent turnaround,
and clears his throat, raises his song in the empty warehouse of autumn.

Translated by Xuan Yuan & Tim Lilburn

清 空

顺着一阵秋风，一辆小汽车
翻了个身，满树叶片突突
发动起返乡运动。一排绿色小乌龟
翻转黄色肚皮在街边顺水漂走，秋天
一声长啸，带着狐狸面具，蹲在树上
坐在河沿，看着感恩节
下午，管理红绿灯的星星
提前下班，一波波小汽车
突突熄火。狐狸把叹息
挂在树叶上，飞去来兮，西风的嘴里
阵阵脆硬苦涩，苦涩莅临，支肘撑起
一场浩大的秋风，盛况，盛况
空前，失语的大师
在秋天的空旷仓库里，华丽转身清理唱腔

Zhao Si (赵四)

Bird Language

Across from the People's Hospital is a small Bird & Flower Market,
secluded as the quarantined hospital during the SARS emergency.

In one of the stores, several sculptural blackbirds
perch idly on tiny branches in their cages,
while around their necks a ring of golden hackles
suggests a sort of noble label "de" or "von".

From the hospital, several masked idlers drop by
and listen to the birds' most requested lines:
"hello" followed by "welcome, welcome, "
their mouths behind masks of open laughter.

One mouth in the crowd speaks affectedly of the birds' tones,
eyes full of lasciviousness — "welcome, welcome."

A long silence,
a long gap in the "caw-caw-caw,"
a blackbird abruptly bursts into strange laughter.

Translated into human speech,
it probably means
"Now, man, you must speak Bird!"

Translated by Xuan Yuan & Tim Lilburn

鸟 语

人民医院对面是个小花鸟市场
非典期间和医院里一样地清静

一家店铺里有几只雕塑般黑鸟
在鸟笼里闲蹲自己细小的树枝
鸟们脖颈间有一圈金黄色羽翎
像“德”或“冯”一类贵族的标记

从医院出来几个戴口罩的闲人
听店主让鸟儿说那著名的台词
“你好”过后是“欢迎光临”
口罩后的嘴们看得出在哈哈开合

其中一张拿捏起鸟的腔调
满眼调戏地——“欢迎光临”

长长的沉默后
“嘎嘎嘎嘎嘎”
鸟儿突然一阵怪笑

翻译成人话
可能是——
“说鸟语了吧，人哪！”

Zhao Si (赵四)

Copying

Wandering in the post-meridian Lotus Market,
I encountered a circle with a cheerful American woman tourist
and a well-trained Chinese male titmouse at the center
their mouths opened at the same time
to a one yuan coin:
"Good Boy!"

The titmouse prudently turns down a dime,
and onlookers from different races
offer their sincere praise
at how he replicates, precisely, human traits.

Translated by Xuan Yuan & Tim Lilburn

拷　贝

游戏在午后的荷花市场
开心的美国女游客和训练有素的中国雄山雀
面对一元硬币一起张嘴
“Good Boy!”

山雀精确地拒绝了一角硬币
围观的各色群众都由衷赞叹
它精确复制的人类价值观

Zhao Si (赵四)

Silver

Praying for nothing except not to be toppled, nothing except not to fall,
nothing except a reed to be raised up when it is bruised,
a smoldering wick that will not be snuffed out intentionally.
Before the age-old curtain of irksome noise is drawn,
a man gradually becomes intimate with a music
of the slow elongating voice of raindrops.
Each and every thread upon sad metal strings
breaks into pieces, spatters still
tears of no return; they are
in the mosaic voices of wheels and axles, pedestrians, traffic signals,
huge flashing screens, steel-concrete buildings, city lights...
modeled on a symphony and drawn randomly a silver world
on the glass walls of each and every skyscraper.

Translated by Xuan Yuan & Tim Lilburn

银

无非是不栽倒，无非是不陨落
无非是祈求芦苇压伤时能有人扶起
灯火未残时不被蓄意吹灭
在岁月烦嚣的声音幕墙里
一个人，日益亲近有着缓缓下落
拉长雨滴声的音乐
一根根闪烁忧伤的金属丝
断了，碎了，还在溅起，
原来是那没有归途的泪水
在轮轴行人交通信号广告屏幕
钢铁灯火混响的城市谐音中
以交响曲为范本在幢幢高楼的
玻璃幕墙上随机画下的银的世界

Zhao Si (赵四)

Sacrificial Flesh

A pair of crumpled, muddy jeans
lies weirdly on the street after the rain
looking like a weather-beaten face.
Are they the aftermath of violence
or simply abandoned clothing?

People with weary faces wait for the bus,
swarm the station to be on time.
When the bus comes, the crowd stirs
as if a flock of raptors dashing toward
sacrificial flesh.

This morning, strangely,
my impaired vision sees
the darkest part of fate that keeps apace
with the scapegoat tied to its doom.

Translated by Xuan Yuan & Bruce Meyer

祭　肉

一条沾满泥、水的揉成团的牛仔裤
不寻常地躺在雨后的街边
像一张饱经风霜的人脸
不知是暴力、伤害的残留物
还是只是简单地被厌弃

一群满脸倦怠的候车人
每天准时地蜂拥在一旁的车站
每当一辆公交车开来
便是一顿乍起，人
仿佛扑向祭肉的鸟群

今天早晨，不寻常地
我的受伤害的视觉，看到
命运最黑暗的部分，总在惦记着
一块不断赶上厄运的祭肉

Zhao Si (赵四)

Autumnal Musing

Like a blade of crabgrass,
the old woman became a fixture at the subway entrance,
over a long winter, a spring, a summer.
Now, autumn has settled.
The woman who crumbles like sandy soil
still holds in her hand tiny flower pots,
mutters, with a trembling voice,
as if squeezed from cracked buildings,
"flowers for sale, flowers for sale..."

On my windowsill,
a small pot of jewel flowers has survived three seasons.
It reminds me silently
with its last plump petals
"Relax, death has its own clock."

Translated by Xuan Yuan & Bruce Meyer

秋　兴

像一株马唐草，
老妇人在地铁站口附生了
至少一冬，一春，一夏
已然入秋了
碎裂成沙土的人
仍端着手中的小小盆花
用仿佛震后建筑物裂缝中挤压出来的声音
抖颤着喃喃：
卖花，卖花……

在我的窗台上
一盆历三季仍在的小小宝石花
用它残存的饱满叶片
静静提醒我：
别紧张，死亡有它自己的钟点

Zhao Si (赵四)

A Beggar with a Skin Disease

In summer,
on the road I take between my workplace and home each day,
is a beggar with a skin-disease. I always encounter him,
ceaselessly scratching his dirty body.

I imagined
by the end of that summer
he would be devoured entirely by fester,
then vanish.

The following autumn,
marvelously, he was still wandering
on the road I take between my workplace and home each day,
scratching no more.

The merciful autumn wind blew away the summer days
and carried with it his despair.

Translated by Xuan Yuan & Bruce Meyer

一个患皮肤病的乞丐

夏日里
在每天上下班的必经之路
我总能遇到一个患皮肤病的乞丐
在不停地抓搔他肮脏的身体

我以为
在夏天结束之前
他就会被溃烂完全吞噬
然后消失

秋天里
他奇迹般地依然徜徉
在我每天上下班的必经之路
并且不再抓搔

仁慈的秋风吹走夏日的时候
也顺带吹走了他的绝望

Zhou Zan (周瓒)

Mr. Zhang San Rides through Town on a Minibus

1.
5p.m. Do what you want to your heart's content. The destination's
unknown: one often meets his sober introspection;
he puts his best foot forward, already knowing
the cost of his travels: what guides him is
an imagined freedom that promptly stops beckoning,
its bargain: mind drills. He gives the hawker

his ferry boat fare. This paragraph requires a path
enriched with imagining; first he seeks out
a seat for his self. Facts of his being on the road needn't
be handed over like those of the official in a picaresque
novel, narrated by an ant army and read by saliva,
knot woven into culture and history by the printing press.

Setting down his drab briefcase,
he shifts his gaze outside the window. His new
p.o.v. replaces the double-sized scorched fantasy photos.
Like a painter who yearns to be a robot,
he'd rather be a speeding camcorder,
discarding a smudged post-Expressionist oil painting.

2.
Please imagine a machine's relaxed mood.
Death, which alters appearances, wields
fragmentary limbs and body, but each part
represents the whole, says, "If it only
listens attentively to death, my entire life
is no life, but suffering." Harboring his cautious

张三先生乘坐中巴穿过本城

1
纵情的下午五点钟。目的地不明
在一生中时时遭遇他冷静反省
他一只脚探出，已经预先
了解到行程的代价：引领他的
是招手即停的想象自由
讨价还价的智力操练。而渡船费

交给吆喝者。一段需要以想象充实的
道路，首先他需要寻找到身份认同
的座位。他“在路上”的事实无需交代
像流浪汉小说中的主人公
被群蚁讲述，被唾沫阅读
被印刷机织进文明和艺术史的网结

现在，放好他那标准牌手提箱
把目光移向窗外。视点的
移动代替梦想中的高倍变焦镜头
像一个画家渴望变成机器人
他也宁愿变成一架摄像机，在飞驰中
留下一片后表现主义的油彩擦痕

2
请想象一架机器的轻松心情
改头换面的死神挥舞着它
残缺的肢体，但每一部分
都能代表整体说话
是的，“如果只是倾听死亡
我的整个生命就不是生命

dread, he returns to people: Li Ke Long's second floor
resembles a weary dyspeptic stomach,
directly across from Shuang An Department Store,
where one pair of huge kids cut from paper emits
intermittent mutters distorted by car horns.

Overpass the stiff underside of a dog's belly,
the road cut up in paperbacks; open the back cover to offer
sacrifices to the blue-clothed god who reads, analyzes, drafts
anew a complete oeuvre on human behavior in ten moralizing
commandments. He thinks his mood is Dante's
entering the forest, as he steps into the exclusive minibus.

3.
"We ourselves become lines of poetry written by books…"
Case in point: at this section of road, we're unable to locate
the imagined components of narrative, a plot.
Alone, the minibus's lyrical rhythm can't lull the post-
industrial masses. He endures his fleeting nature at the bus-
stop, as if it were a self-indulgent fever.

Bus stops: Taiping Zhuang, Nonglin Ju, Madian, Jing'an Zhuang:
they're either the city's mosquitoes or fluttering characters
in the midst of a crowd's raucousness; yet this silk brush
might as well stop him from using women around him
to bear the complicated experience of the gaze. He, Mr. Zhang San,
an ordinary man, is possessed of some natural rights.

"Among women, who is most fond of shopping where: Qiancun Department
Store, Instec, or the Lufthansa Center?" You can only guess
by the clothing…his darling wife stays at home, and she knows
her women's hobbies; one among these women was in love with traitor
Yu Yongze; his arrest stems from his dear gluttonous wife's hobby.

而是苦难”。怀着审慎的恐惧
他回到人们中间：利客隆的二楼
像一只疲惫的消化不良的胃
正向着对面的双安商场那一对
巨幅民间剪纸式的孩童发出
被汽车喇叭篡改的断断续续的嘟哝

过街天桥僵瘦的犬腹下
道路被分割成等级制的现代平装本
书籍，打开后可供永恒的蓝衣上帝
阅读、分析，重新制定一整套关于
人类行为道德的十诫。他想象
他是以但丁进入丛林的心情踏上了中巴

3
“我们自身就成了正在被书写的诗行……”
这段道路就是例证，找不到任何
可以设想为叙事的情节成份
中巴式的抒情节奏不适合单独面对
后工业时代的大众。他忍受临时性
停车的分行就像忍受激情的放纵

太平庄、农林局、马甸和静安庄
都市中的蚊子或文字飞舞在
噪音的众声喧哗之间；而这丝毫
也不妨碍他使得周围的女性
承受被看的复杂体验。他，张三先生
一个面貌普通的男人的天赋人权

“她们中间谁最热衷于购物，仟村百货
英斯泰克还是燕莎商城？”只能从
衣着上猜想……他家有贤妻，对于
女士们的爱好算是有经验，她们中的一位
爱上叛徒余永泽，就为他的被捕
出自一个与贪吃有关的贤妻的爱好

4.
Parcel of pig liver and confidential Party materials, love or
revolutionary enterprise,
these are antitheses in the books he's read;
the question he has no time for allegorized
by passengers getting on and off in turn: "Those who want to get on, get on;
if it's your stop, say something"—history's meaning
found in excessive annotations of ordinary speech.

But why must his identity be made clear?
Why does the author not want to discover something about him he cannot find?
He takes a calculator from his briefcase, checks
how much his business has earned.
His youth is promising; is his seat on the minibus
nothing more than a mark of the nouveau riche?

"Will have bread, will have everything." He admires
the Marlboro pressed between his fingers, distinguished emblem
of two esteemed cultures, characters: Act! Victory lies ahead! Yet he
identifies himself with the cigarette: "I am being burned
to the utmost degree by my own flame
and curl up in my smoke."

5.
"She left home beneath a cloud."
Now he can't not remember his old love;
this boring era couldn't propagate
the complex desires of postcoloniality: not missing a beat,
Private Second Class Wang Er brings back the past,
like a cigarette's anger and depression;
now elsewhere, she plays the lover's role.

At that time they were thought happily earnest (which, according
to some definitions means "sincere"); it's all been done
before: romance, jealousy, self-pity, hateful eyes, the begging,
giving up no more than indifference with verbs and adjectives-
the emotions they manipulate, keywords of an adolescent thesis.

4
一包猪肝与党的机要，爱情或革命事业
在他阅读过的书籍中构造着对立
他无暇自我论争的问题正被轮流更替
的乘客隐喻着："想上的上来了
到了地儿的就该言语一声"——历史真谛
就在对于日常语言的过度诠释中

而为什么他得是个身份明确的角色
写作者对他什么也不想演绎，也做不到
他从手提箱里拿出计算器，算一算
他最近的一笔生意能挣得多少
他年轻有为，坐在中巴里也顶多
是个准中产阶级的暴发户？

"面包会有的，一切都会有的"。他赞赏
他夹着万宝路的食指和中指分别代表的
两个国际性的文化雅号：操！胜利在望！而他
把自己准确地定位在香烟的位置
"我正在被我自己的火焰燃尽
并被我自己的烟雾缭绕"

5
"她在一朵云下离开了家"
现在他不能不回忆起他的一个旧情人
这种无聊的时候还能不滋生
后殖民心态的复杂欲望：二等兵王二
不失时机地提醒他往事如烟的愤闷
她如今在地球的另一端扮作情人

幸运的是那时候他们还算认真，而从
某种意义上讲，认真即真诚
一切都已出演了一遍：浪漫、嫉妒
自怜、仇视、乞求、放弃乃至无所谓
由动词和形容词操纵感情世界
成为他们最典型的青春期论文关键词

But always the body first summons wisdom,
prolegomenon of phenomena's ultimate proposition,
inferior to imagination's pleasures as it arrives at the other shore.
Sublimated to her form, however blurred, he draws
the support of a few images: is one woman not all
women? But is he himself?

6.
He savors abstract rain water in the concrete wind:
"If oceans are doomed to break dams, let
the bitter waters empty into my heart."
In an instant, he sees his hand holding a spear;
he charges the enemy position,
Rocinante swerves with astonishing speed,
his misconceived Terminator screams sweeping past
the small hotel and food stalls beside the road.

He stretches. "Our sleep, our hunger." The corner turns,
he gallops outside God's reasoned commandments, the field of civil rule
colored lights that wind around branches, like ads on public billboards
lining up to guard the country's great festivals.
"The world related to me, oh!"
But who, based on his immaculate dress, gleans his classical
view of the whole world? Odysseus is finally returning home.

Getting along in years, nearing death in a scenic poem,
Mr. Zhang San gets off at Nongzhan Guan, changes buses,
jumps on another minibus;
after half an hour, the mousy-haired missus opens the many-locked door
and greets him—the color of the sky darkened long ago, maze of asphalt debauched
with red lanterns, green wine;
in the next poem he encounters Mephistopheles, but for now
he shakes off the glare of three lights at the intersection, following
me as I trudge into
night's dim territory.

Translated by Susan M. Schultz & Jennifer Feeley

不过总还是肉体的召唤先于存在
的哲思；现象学的终极命题不及一次
想象中的快感所抵达的彼岸。过犹不及
她的形象却已模糊了，只好借助
一些概念化的图像升华：一个女人不就是
所有的女人？而他是他自己吗？

6
他在具体的风中品尝抽象的雨水
“如果海洋注定要决堤，就让
所有的苦水都注入我心中”
一瞬间他仿佛看见自己手执长矛，冲锋陷阵
弩辛难得晃动着惊人的速度，以终结者
怒吼的错觉，掠过路边的小旅馆和大排档

伸展“我们的睡眠，我们的饥饿”。它拐弯
驰入上帝戒律的法外情，公民规章的试验田
彩灯缠绕树枝，与公益广告牌一同
列队守卫国家的重大节日。“与我相关的世界啊！”
而谁将从他衣冠楚楚的品牌中辨认出
古典的整体性世界观？俄底修斯终将回家

年老、死亡，在一首场景式诗歌中
张三先生从农展馆下车，倒车跳上另一辆中巴
半小时后，鸡窝头的老婆会打开防盗门
迎接他一天色早已昏暗，城市丛林灯红酒绿
下一首诗将记载他遭遇靡非斯陀，而此刻
摆脱路口那三色灯的瞪视，他随我步入夜色

CONTRIBUTORS

POETS

An Qi (安琪, 1969–), pen name of Huang Jiang Pin, was born in in Zhangzhou, Fu Jian Province. She writes poetry and other literary works. She sometimes paints as well. She is a member of China Writers' Association and one of the Top Ten Female Youth of the new century. Her co-edited books are *The Third Said* and *Complete Works by the Middle Generation Poets*. Her published collections of poetry include *The Running Fence*, *You Cannot Imitate My Life*, *The Polar Region*, and *Notes of Feminist.*

Chen Dongdong (陈东东, 1961–) was born in Shanghai and graduated from the Shanghai Normal University in 1984. He studied Chinese Language and Literature and began writing poetry during his college years. He is widely regarded as one of the leading poets of the Chinese Contemporary Poetry movement. Chen has been the editor of *Works* (1982-1984), *Tendency* (1988-1991), and *Southern Poetry Magazine* (1992-1994). He was also the poetry editor of the overseas literary and humanities journal *Tendency* (1994-1997). His publications include a book of long poems, *Summer book – Unblocked Book* (2018); two collections of short poems, *Guide Map* (2013) and *The Night of the Sea God* (2018); a volume of hybrid writing, *Flowing Water* (2018); and two books of essays, *Black Mirror* (2013) and *Thoughts on Poetry* (2013). With Chinese American poet Zhang Er, he co-edited a bilingual anthology of Chinese contemporary poetry, *Another Kind of Nation: An Anthology of Contemporary Chinese Poetry* (Talisman House, 2007).

Chen Li (陈黎,1954–) was born in Hualien, Taiwan, and received his B.A. in English from Taiwan Normal University. Regarded as one of the most innovative and exciting poets writing in Chinese today, he has published 15 books of poetry and is also a prolific prose writer and translator. In 2012, he represented Taiwan at the Olympic Poetry Festival (Poetry Parnassus) in London. In 2014, he was invited to participate in the International Writing Program at the University of Iowa.

Che Qianzi (车前子, 1963–), pen name of Gu Pan, is a Chinese poet, essayist, and painter born in Suzhou, P.R. of China and currently resides in Beijing. Publications include over 30 collections of poems and essays: *The New Rider and Horse*, *Inventions*, *Fortune-Telling*, and *Respectability*. His motto is "The self as reflected in a poet's selections is nothing but a piece of art."

Gao Xing (高兴, 1963–) was born in the Jiangsu Province of China and graduated from Beijing Foreign Studies University in 1987. He is the author of several books of essays and hundreds of poems. He has also translated Milan Kundera, Ivan Klima, Marin Sorescu,

Nichita Stanescu, Ana Blandiana, Ismail Kadare, Tomaz Salamun, and many others. He is currently editor in chief of *World Literature*, a renowned journal in China.

Huang Fan (黄梵, 1963–) is a leading writer of poetry and fiction, known for his unflinching confrontation of contemporary issues in China with dry humor and dark lyricism. His books in Chinese include *Moon Losting Sleeping*, *Elegies of Nanjing*, *The Eleventh Commandment*, *The Floating Colors*, *Until Youth Disappears*, *Girls' School Teacher*, and *Chinese Wander*. "Middle Age" was included in *One Hundred Poems for One Hundred Years of Chinese Modern Poetry*. His prizes include the Boao International Poetry Prize, the China Good Poetry Prize, the Beijing Literary Prize for Poetry, the Jinling Literary Prize for Poetry, the Fangcao Biennial Top Ten Prize for Poetry, the Zijin Mountain Literature Prize, and the Writer's Golden Prize for Short Story. His poetry has been featured in *Push Open the Window* (Copper Canyon 2011) *Poetry*, and *A Public Space* and has been praised by English-language poets aesthetically diverse as Robert Hass, Ron Padgett, and J.H. Prynne. His works have been translated into English, Italian, German, Greek, French, Japanese, Farsi, and Korean.

Huang Lihai (黄礼孩, 1975–) was born in Xuwen, the town farthest south on the Chinese mainland, and now lives in Guangzhou. His poems have been collected in more than a hundred anthologies. He has published a number of books of poems, including *I Know Little about Life* and *The Passionate Mazurkaand* as well as volumes of criticism on art, dance, film, and poetry. He has won a number of prizes, including the 8th Lu Xun Literary Award (Guangzhou, 2009) and Lebanon International Literary Award (2013). Huang established the poetry magazine *Poetry & People* in 1999 and the *Poetry & People* Poet Prize in 2005 which has been awarded to Adam Zagajewski, Tomaž Šalamun, and Tomas Tranströmer.

Hu Mingming (胡茗茗, 1967–) is a member of China Writers Association, a poet, and scriptwriter enrolled by the 23rd Youth Poetry Meeting organized by the *Poetry Periodical Magazine* and the 22nd Study Program held by Lu Xun Literary Institute. She was awarded the 2010 China Writers Publishing House Prize, the 3rd Chinese Women Literature Prize, the 11th Renaissance Prize of Hebei Province, the 4th Taiwan Maple Leaf Prize, and the title of Outstanding Poet of *Selected Poems Magazine*. She has published four books of poetry including *Yoga Poems* and *Genuine Poems*. Her literary works have been published by many authoritative periodicals including *People's Literature* and *Poetry Periodical Magazine*.

Jiang Tao (姜涛, 1970–) currently teaches in the Department of Chinese at Peking University. He began writing poetry in 1990 and devoted himself to poetry criticism and researching the history of poetry in the Twentieth Century. His publications include, among others, the poetry collections *Book of Birds*, *The Good News*, *The Wonderful World We Live To-*

gether, the critical volume, *Bakunin's Hands*, and the scholarly works: *The Tower in Apartment, Anthologies*, and the *Emergence of Modern Chinese Poetry*.

Lan Lan (蓝蓝, 1967–) has ten volumes of poetry that have appeared in Chinese, six essay collections, and numerous fairytales. Born in Yantai, Shandong Province, she began publishing at 14. She is one of the most celebrated contemporary Chinese poets whose lyrical work has been rendered into a dozen languages in various international venues. Her many awards include the Liu Li'an Poetry Prize, the *Poetry and People's* Annual Prize, and the Yuan Kejia Poetry Prize. Her *From Here to Here: New & Selected Poems*, edited and translated by Diana Shi and George O'Connell, is seeking a U.S. publisher. Attracted to classical Greek myth and history, she has been named an honorary citizen of Chios, and her poetic drama *Borders* was recently performed in Athens. She has been a visiting professor at several institutions and Poet-In-Residence at Renmin University. She lives in Beijing.

Li Shaojun (李少君, 1967–) is a native of Xiangxiang, Hunan Province, and graduated from Wuhan University with a major in Journalism. Once the chief editor of *Tianya*, he is currently the associate editor in chief of *Poetry Journal*. His books of poetry include *Nature Collection*, *Grass Root Collection*, and *Blue Bar*. He is acclaimed as the "Poet of the Natural World."

Ouyang Jianghe (欧阳江河, 1956–) played a central role in the 1980s underground Sichuanese poetry scene that gave rise to the Chinese poetic avant-garde when became known as one of the "Five Masters from Sichuan." Since then he has emerged as one of China's most prominent literary figures, authoring four books of poetry and essays and publishing numerous works of criticism on art, music, and literature. He is also a noted calligrapher. In 2010, he was awarded the Chinese Literature Media Award for poetry. He lives in Beijing and travels frequently to the U.S. and Germany. *Doubled Shadows* is his debut poetry collection in English.

Potato Brother (马铃薯兄弟, 1962–) was born in a village in Donghai, Jiangsu Province, China. One of the most important poets of China's "Middle Generation," he has written under the pen name Potato Brother since the 1980s. After studying Chinese Literature at East China Normal University, he began widespread publication. His poems have been collected in many anthologies and translated into English and French. He currently works as a literature editor for Phoenix Publishing & Media Group (PPMG) publishing house. He has been voted "The Best Editor in China."

Shen Qi (沈奇, 1951–) is a poet and poetry critic. She is currently a professor in the literature department at Xi'an University of Finance and Economics and a member of the Peking University Poetry Research Institute.

Shu Yu (舒羽, 1979–) is a contemporary poet, writer, and founder of the International Grand Canal Poetry Festival (since 2012) in Hangzhou. She was born in Tonglu, a small town of Zhejiang Province. Having received traditional Chinese music training from maestros, she had been a TV host for some years. Recently, she is running Shu Yu Cafe, a coffee shop on the theme of culture. She writes in her spare time. Her works are known for their "diversity, spiritualism and dynamism." Her publications include a poetry collection *Poems of Shu Yu* (Writers Publishing House in Mainland China, 2010 / Sanyi Culture, 2011), a prose collection *Flowing Water* (Writers Publishing House in Mainland China, 2013 / INK Literature in Taiwan, 2014), and an anthology of poetry and prose *Being a Snail Full of Details* (Zhejiang Literary and Art Publishing House, 2015).

Sun Dong (孙冬, 1969–) is a professor at Nanjing University of Finance and Economics. She graduated from Nanjing University with a PhD in English literature. Her works include a monograph, *Against Interpretation: on the Indeterminacy of Sam Shepard's Theater*, and two poetry books, *The Cruel Crow* (with Dong Feng) and *The Broken Crow*. She edited the book *Reciprocal Translation Project* (Roof). Her poems have been translated into French, English, Turkish, and Romanian and published in various literary magazines, newspapers, and other online media outlets. She won the second Lu Zhu Award for Poetry in 2018.

Tian Yuan (田原, 1965–) was born in the Henan Province. Earning his doctorate in Japanese Literature from Ritsumeikan University, he currently teaches at Josai International University. His main publications include the Chinese volumes *Selected Poems of Tian Yuan* and *A Snake in Dreams*, the Chinese-English bilingual volume *Beijing-Tokyo Poems Composition*, and in Japanese, *Thus the Shore Was Born*, *Memory in Stone*, *A Snake in Dreams*, and *Selected Poems of Tian Yuan*. His translations include *Selected Poems of Tanikawa Shuntarō* (published in 16 volumes in Chinese), *Selected Poems of Tsutsumi Seiji*, *Selected Poems of Takahashi Mutsuo*, *Complete Works of Kaneko Misuzu*, and more. He has edited volumes such as *Tanikawa Shuntarō: Selected Poems: Volumes 1-4* (published by Shūeisha Bunko), his doctoral dissertation, *Theorizing Tanikawa Shuntarō* (published by Iwanami Shoten), and others. In 2001, he was awarded the first Foreign Student Poetry Prize and in 2010, the 60th annual Mr. H Award. He received the 2013 10th annual Shanghai Literature Award, the 2015 Overseas Chinese Poets Award, and the first annual Taiwan Pacific Translation Award in 2017. His works have also been published in Mongolian and Korean translation.

Un Sio San (袁绍珊, 1985–) is a poet and writer. She has attained dual bachelor's degrees in Chinese and Literature and Art from Peking University, as well as dual master's degrees in East Asian Studies and Asia-Pacific Studies from the University of Toronto. She has won the Henry Luce Foundation Chinese Poetry Award (U.S.), The China Times Literature Awards (Taiwan), and the Macao Literary Award to name a few. In 2014, she was the poet-in-residence at the Vermont Studio Center (U.S.). She has been invited to many international poetry festivals, including New York and Lisbon. She was the lyricist of Macao's first original chamber opera *A Fragrant Dream*. Her poetry collections include *Evolution of Love*, *Wonderland*, and *A Bustle Island – Article Collections from Hong Kong, Taiwan and Macao*.

Wang Jiaxin (王家新, 1957–) was born in the Hubei Province of China. He was "sent down" after high school to do hard labor in the countryside during the Cultural Revolution. He later studied literature at Wuhan University and became a teacher and literary editor. He is currently a literature professor at Renmin University of China in Beijing. Eminent among contemporary Chinese poets and essayists, he has received numerous awards, and his works have been selected for major anthologies and college textbooks in China. His was a former Luce Poet-in-Residence at Colgate University and the 2013 resident poet of International Writing Program at University of Iowa. He has authored more than 50 collections of poetry and essays and is a prolific anthologist. *Gotland's Dusk*, his selected volume of poetry in German, was published in 2011. *Darkening Mirror*, his full-length volume of poetry in English with a foreword written by Robert Hass, was published in 2016. He is also a winner of the 4th Changwon KC International Poetry and Literature Award in 2017.

Wang Xiaoni (王小妮, 1955–) was born in Chang Chun, China. She spent seven years farming in the countryside during the Cultural Revolution. In 1982, Xiaoni graduated from Jilin University and then worked as an editor at Chang Chun Film Studio. In 1985, she settled in Shenzen and became a professor at Hainan University. She has published over 25 books of poetry including *My Selected Poems* (1986), *Exile in Shenzhen* (1994), *My Paper Wraps My Fire* (1997), *Something Crosses My Mind* (2014) *To the Other World* (2013) , among others as well as many essays, short stories and novels. Wang has received numerous awards, including the second annual Chinese Literature Media Award in 2004. In 2015, the translation of her book *Something Crosses My Mind* by Eleanor Goodman was shortlisted for the International Griffin Poetry Prize.

Xiao Xiao (潇潇, 1964–) is a poet, painter, and editor in chief of *Chinese Poetry Online*. Her works have been translated into German, English, Persian, Arabic, Bengali, and Spanish. Her paintings have been included in exhibits such as the *Exhibit of Contemporary Chinese Poets* and the *Contemporary Chinese Literati Painting and Calligraphy Exhibit*. Her long poem, "Elegy for Another World," was named one of the masterpieces of Chinese women's literature in the 1990s and was translated into English and published in full in *Long Poem Magazine* in Cambridge, England in May 2018. Xiao Xiao won the Wenchuan Earthquake Relief Outstanding Volunteer Award in 2008. She has won a number of poetry awards in China and abroad, including the Wen Yiduo Poetry Award, One Hundred Years of New Poetry Special Contribution Award, Poetry Tide Annual Poetry Award, Beijing Literature Poetry Award, *China Poetry Net* Top Ten Excellent Poems 2017, Top Ten Poets 2018, Romania Algezi International Literature Prize. Xiao Xiao is the first Asian to have won that award, and she was awarded an honorary Romanian citizenship.

Yang Ke (杨克, 1957–) is a representative poet of the Third Generation and the Folk Writing Position. He is the author of 11 collections of Chinese poems, four collections of essays, and a book of collected works. His representative poetry collections include *Poems of Yang Ke*, *Relevant and Irrelevant*, and *I Spoke Out the Shape of the Wind*. His poems have appeared in 400 poetry anthologies including the *Chinese New-vernacular Literature Collection* and the *Centenary of Chinese New Poetry*. His poems have been translated into various foreign languages including English, Japanese, and Spanish, and he has published several poetry collections in the U.S., Japan, and Spain. He is the editor in chief of multiple poetry anthologies including *China New Poem Almanac*, *Selected Poems of "They" of the Last Decade*, and *A Hundred New Poems for Children*. He is the recipient of numerous national literature awards and foreign poetry awards including the Xu Zhimo Poetry Award of the University of Cambridge, Outstanding Poet Award of Romanian Publishing House, Lu Xun Art Award of Guangdong, and First Biennial Award for Best Ten Poets. He has held individual poetry and calligraphy exhibitions in Shenzhen Art Gallery and other galleries. He is a member of the presidium of the Chinese Writers Association, a vice president of Chinese Poetry Society, and the proprietor of *Works* literary journal. He is also the judge of the top Chinese Literature Award, the Mao Dun Literature Award, and the deputy director of the juries of Lu Xun Literature Award in poetry.

Yao Feng (姚风, 1958–), pen name of Yao Jingming, was born in Beijing. He studied Portuguese in Beijing and is currently a full professor at the University of Macau. He has published widely in poetry, translation, and prose. In addition to writing Chinese poetry, he also writes in Portuguese and translates Portuguese poems into Chinese. He was the winner of the 14th Rougang Poetry Award in 2004 and was awarded Ordem Militar de Santiago de Espada by the President of Portugal in 2006. In 2009, he curated the installation exhibition *Belonging*.

Yen Ai-Lin (颜艾琳, 1968–) was born in Tainan, Taiwan in 1968. She holds a degree in History from Fu Jen Catholic University and has studied in the M.A. program of Language and Creative Writing at National Taipei University of Education. During her youth, she played bass for a punk rock band, performed in an experimental theater, and was a member of *Kindle* poetry quarterly and many other indie magazines. She is a consultant for the New Taipei City Government, Cardinal Tien Educational Center. As an active member of the international literary scene, she is the Taiwanese consultant for *Poetry Review*, a Korean literary quarterly. She also consults and writes articles for poetry magazines and online media outlets in Mainland China. In her fruitful career as a poet, she has won many major literary awards, including the 2010 Wu Cho-liu Literary Awards for new poetry, the 2011 Chinese Literature and Art Literary Award, the Outstanding Youth Publishing Award, the National Outstanding Poet Award, Poet Laureate of Hainan Island Poetry Festival, Poet Laureate of the Reciter Poetry Festival, and her works were selected as the optimal poems by the *Epoch Poetry Quarterly* for their 14th anniversary.

Yu Bang (育邦, 1976–) is engaged in poetry, fiction, and literary critical writing. He has written the short stories "Goodbye, Beetles" and "Panamanian Panties," the literary essays "The Prowler," "Arty Types," "From Joyce to Marquez," and the poetry collections *War within the Body* and *Memoir of My Old Friends*. He is one of the representative poets of the 70s generation in China. He lives in the city of Nanjing.

Zhai Yongming (翟永明, 1955–) was born in Chengdu, Sichuan. As a teenager during the Cultural Revolution, she spent time in a village. Her earliest poems were published in 1981, her first collection appeared four years later, and many more books have followed. Her style continues to evolve, and she is active in women's poetry and the arts. She co-owns a bar in Chengdu called White Nights, which has functioned for over a decade as an informal salon for local writers and artists.

Zang Di (臧棣, 1964–) is a poet, critic, translator, and editor born in Beijing. He was admitted to Chinese Department of Peking University in September 1983 and received a PhD in Literature from Peking University in July 1997, where he has been teaching since 1996, and is currently a professor in the Chinese Department and editor of the journal *New Poetry Criticism*. He worked briefly as a journalist for China News Agency from 1990 to 1993. He has won numerous poetic prizes and awards including Pearl River International Poetry Festival Award in 2007, the Perfect Chinese Literature Award from Changjiang River Literature & Art in 2008, and Poet of the Year 2008 by the Chinese Literature Media Awards. His many honors include one of Contemporary China's Top Ten Prominent Young Poets (2005), 1979-2005 China's Top Ten Avant-Courier Poets (2006), China's Top Ten Rising Poetry Critics (2007), Contemporary China's Top Ten Rising Poets (2007), and Chinese Poetry Biennial Top Ten Poets (2008). He is the author of several collections of poetry including *Memory of Yan Yuan* (1998), *The Rustle of Leaves in the Wind* (2000), *Fresh Thorns* (2002), *The Universe is Flat* (2008), and *Empty-City Strategy* (2009).

Zhang Zhihao (张执浩,1965–) was born in Jingmen, the Hubei Province. He is editor in chief of *Chinese Poetry* and lives in the city of Wuhan. His main works include the anthologies of poetry, *Hard to Praise*, *Broadness*, *Wild Flowers on the Plateau*, and other novels and short story collections. He has won the People's Literature Prize, the Chinese Literature Media Award for poet of the year 2013, the Chen Zi-ang Poetry Prize, founded by the nationwide magazine *Poetry*, and the Lu Xun Literature Prize, the most prestigious literary prize in China.

Zhao Si (赵四, 1972–) is a Chinese poet, essayist, translator, poetics scholar, editor, and either the author or translator of 11 books, including *White Crow* (Poems, 2005), *Gold-in-Sand Picker* (Prose Poems, 2005), *Disappearing, Recalling: 2009–2014 New Selected Poems* (2016), which won the "2014 Major Support Project" by China Writers Association,

Matchstick Man (in U.S., 2017, nominated for the 42nd Pushcart Poetry Prize), *Zmiznutia a návraty* (in Slovakia, 2018, the first contemporary Chinese poet's book published in Slovakia), two poetry books of Tomaž Šalamun (both 400+ pages each): *Light-Blue-Pillow Tower* (2014) and *The Enormous Boiling Mouths of the Sun* (2016), *Edmond Jabès: Complete Poems* (one of two translators, 2019), and the selected work of others: Hart Crane (US), Ted Hughes (UK), Vladimir Holan (Czech), Yannis Ritsos (Greece), et al. Her poetry has been translated into 16 languages and published worldwide. She works for *Poetry Periodical*, the top poetry magazine in China, and is the executive editor-in-chief of the prestigious poetry translation series *Contemporary International Poetry*. She was awarded the Polish Marii Konopnickiej Poetry Prize in 2012. She was an Orion Visiting Artist in University of Victoria, Canada in 2017.

Zhou Zan (周瓒, 1968–) is a poet, translator, playwright and literature scholar. Her main works include the poetry collections *Turn Me Loose* and *Another Life of Ne-Zha* and the critical essays "Through the Periscope of Poetic Writing" and "After Shaking off Silence." Her translations include Nina Cassian's *Cheerleader for a Funeral* and Margaret Atwood's *Eating Fire: Selected Poetry 1965-1995*. She lives in Beijing and works for the Chinese Academy of Social Sciences.

TRANSLATORS

Bei Ta, born in Jiangsu Province, now lives in Beijing and serves the National Museum of Modern Chinese Literature as a professional poet, critic, and translator. He has published around 30 books including the poetry book *Rusting Hour Hands*, poetics book *Lightening One's Own Abyss—a Selection of Essays on Poetics*, and the translation of *A Selection of Rabindranath Tagore's Poems*. His poetry manuscripts are collected by the Shanghai Municipal Library.

Chang Fen-ling received her B.A. in English from Taiwan Normal University. A prolific literary critic and award-winning translator, she has translated Chinese over twenty volumes of poetry into Chinese with her husband Chen Li including the works of Sylvia Plath, Carol Ann Duffy, César Vallejo, Pablo Neruda, Octavio Paz, Wisława Szymborska, Matsuo Basho, and Kobayashi Issa.

Chen Hongbo was born in 1988 and comes from Yichang, Hubei Province of China. She is now a PhD candidate of English literature at the School of Foreign Languages, Central China Normal University, as well as a lecturer at Hubei University.

Chen Xing holds a PhD of Comparative Literature. She now lives in Chongqing, teaching English and literature at the Sichuan Fine Arts Institute.

Jonathan Chiang is a freelance translator and writer. He was born in Taipei, Taiwan, in 1994. He obtained a master's degree in translation at The Chinese University of Hong Kong and currently lives in Hong Kong. Several of his works can be found in *A Journey on Foot*.

Jennifer Feeley holds a PhD in East Asian Languages and Literature from Yale University. Her translations of poetry and prose from Chinese into English have been published in numerous journals and anthologies. She is the co-editor of *Simultaneous Worlds: Global Science Fiction Cinema* and the recipient of a Luce Foundation Chinese Poetry and Translation Fellowship.

Eleanor Goodman's book of translations, *Something Crosses My Mind: Selected Poems of Wang Xiaoni* (Zephyr Press, 2014) was the recipient of a 2013 PEN/Heim Translation Grant and winner of the 2015 Lucien Stryk Prize. The book was also shortlisted for the International Griffin Prize. Her first collection of poetry, *Nine Dragon Island* (Enclave/Zephyr, 2016), was a finalist for the *Drunken Boat* First Book Prize. She is a research associate at Harvard's Fairbank Center for Chinese Studies.

Jia Yun resides in Georgia, writing news assignments for an Atlanta-based Chinese website and tutoring Mandarin Chinese as a second language.

Shelley Kristina Hu is a member of the Academy of American Poets and Illinois State Poetry Society, President of Windy City Poet Association, and an Associate Chair of Meihua Culture Club. Her poetry works have been published in books and journals in the U.S. and abroad.

Kit Kelen is a well-known Australian poet, scholar, and visual artist and an English professor at the University of Macau, where he has taught creative writing and literature for the last sixteen years. Volumes of his poetry have been published in Chinese, Portuguese, French, Italian, Swedish, Indonesian and Filipino. Japanese and Greek collections are currently in preparation. The most recent of his dozen English language poetry books is *Scavengers Season*, published by Puncher and Wattmann in 2014.

Karen Kun graduated from University of Macao and holds a BA in English Studies.

Benjamin Landauer is a poet and translator from San Francisco. He graduated with a BA from Reed College in 2017 and is currently pursuing his MA in Chinese Literature at Nanjing University. He has previously studied at Fujian Normal University and Beijing Minzu University. His Chinese poetic compositions have appeared in *Youth* and his Chinese critical essays have appeared in *Youth, China Publishing and Media Journal*, and *Art Panorama.* His literary interests are broad, partial to both modern and classical literature.

Liang Yujing is a poet and translator who has translated hundreds of poems from English into Chinese. Currently lives in New Zealand.

Li Yiliang is a Chinese poet, translator, and critic of poetry. He was born in a small country village in central China at the beginning of the so-called Culture Revolution. After graduating from the Central China Normal University, located in the City of Wuhan on the Yangtze River, he has taught English language and literature in a professional institute for over ten years. He is now an administrative clerk working for China Telecom. His creative writings and translations have won him several prizes and have been awarded by some prestigious publishing organizations. His collection of poetry, *Against the Current*, published by Chongqing University Press in 2009. His translations of Polish, German, American and Canadian poetry have appeared in many publications in China. His anthology of Adam Zagajewski's poetry translated into Chinese is in print. Li lives in the City of Wuhan with his family.
Tim Lilburn was born in Regina, Saskatchewan, Canada. He has published ten books of poetry, including *To the River* (1999), *Kill-site* (2003), *Orphic Politics* (2008), *Assiniboia* (2012), and two books of essays, both concerned with poetics, eros and politics, especially

environmentalism, *Living in the World as if It Were Home* (1999) and *Going Home* (2008). His work has received a Canada's Governor General's Award (for *Kill-site*), the Saskatchewan Book of the Year Award, and the Canadian Authors Association Award among other prizes. He also has edited and contributed to two influential essay anthologies on poetics, *Poetry and Knowing* and *Thinking and Singing: Poetry and the Practice of Philosophy*. He has been a writer-in-residence at the University of Western Ontario, the University of Alberta, and St. Mary's University, as well as the Regina Public Library, and now teaches in the Department of Writing at the University of Victoria. His work has been widely translated and anthologized.

Andrea Lingenfelter is a poet, translator, and scholar of Chinese literature. Her published translations include *The Changing Room: Selected Poetry of Zhai Yongming* (Northern California Book Award winner) and Hon Lai Chu's collection of surrealistic short fiction *The Kite Family* (NEA Translation Fellowship grantee). Her translations of contemporary Chinese-language poetry and fiction have been published in *Manoa*, *Granta*, *Chinese Literature Today*, *Pathlight*, *Zoland Poetry Annual*, *Words Without Borders*, *Asian CHA*, *Two Lines*, and elsewhere. She is also the translator of Li Pik-wah's (Lilian Lee) *Farewell My Concubine* and *The Last Princess of Manchuria*, and *Candy* by Mian Mian. A two-time recipient of Vermont Studio Center Luce Translation Fellowships, she is currently putting together a book-length collection of her translations of Luce Fellowship partner Wang Yin's poetry. Other projects include a translation of Zhai Yongming's book-length poem *Following Huang Gongwang Through the Fuchun Mountains* and Wang Anyi's multigenerational historical novel *Scent of Heaven*. Her own poetry has appeared in *Asian CHA* and *Strix*. She teaches literature and translation at the University of San Francisco.

Liu Qianqian is a PhD candidate from the School of Chinese Language and Literature at Central China Normal University. Her study focuses on comparative literature and world literature.

Liu Xuelan is a professor at the Foreign Literature Institute, Chinese Academy of Social Sciences. She has translated and published five books from English into Chinese. She now lives in Beijing.

Denis Mair holds an M.A. in Chinese from Ohio State University and has taught as a lecturer at Whitman College and the University of Pennsylvania. He was a research fellow for many years at Hanching Academy. He is currently a translation consultant for Zhongkun Cultural Fund, Beijing and serves as a translator for Jidi Majia (Secretary-of-Secretariat, Chinese Writers Association). Denis translated books by the Buddhist monk Shih Chen-hua (SUNY Albany Press, 1992), the philosopher Feng Youlan (Hawaii University Press, 2000), and the art critic Zhu Zhu (Hunan Fine Arts Press, 2009). His poetry translations include *Frontier*

Taiwan (Columbia University Press, 2005), *Contemporary Chinese Poetry* (Shanghai Literary Arts Press, 2007), *Yan Zhi, Reading the Times* (Homa & Sekey Books, 2012), *Jidi Majia, Rhapsody in Black* (Univ. of Oklahoma, 2014), *Jidi Majia, Shade of Our Mountain Range* (Mkhiva Foundation, 2014), *Jidi Majia, From the Snow Leopard to Mayakovsky* (Kallatumba Press, 2017), and *Yang Ke, Two Halves of the World Apple* (Univ. of Oklahoma Press, 2017). He has also translated poetry by Yan Li, Meng Lang and many others. He has written his own poetry collection *Man Cut in Wood,* published by Valley Contemporary Poets (Los Angeles, 2004).

Bruce Meyer is the author or editor of sixty-three books of poetry, short fiction, non-fiction, literary journalism, memoir, portrait photographs, textbooks, and reference books. He received his PhD from McMaster University before receiving a Social Sciences and Humanities Research Council of Canada Post-Doctoral Fellowship. His broadcasts on the *Great Books, Great Poetry*, and *A Novel Idea* for CBC Radio with Michael Enright remain the network's bestselling spoken-word CD series, and his books, *The Golden Thread: A Reader's Journey Through the Great Books* and *Portraits of Canadian Writers* were national bestsellers. He is a two-time winner of the Gwendolyn MacEwen Prize for Poetry and the E.J. Pratt Gold Medal and Prize for Poetry. He has also won the Woolf Poetry Prize in Switzerland, the Ruth Cable Memorial Prize, and the IP Silver Medal for Best Book of Poems in North America in 2014 for *The Seasons*. He was the inaugural Poet Laureate of the City of Barrie and lives there. He teaches at Georgian College and is a Fellow of Victoria College in the University of Toronto where he teaches creative writing and comparative literature.

George O'Connell is an American poet and translator. He has taught creative writing and literature in both American and Chinese universities, serving as Fulbright professor at Peking University and National Taiwan University. In addition to numerous U.S. honors for his poetry, including the Pablo Neruda Prize, he has received a U.S. National Endowment for the Arts Literature Fellowship in Translation as well as Hong Kong Arts Development Council awards. He and Diana Shi co-direct *Pangolin House*, an international journal of Chinese and English-language poetry and art.

Ouyang Yu, now based in Melbourne, came to Australia in mid-April 1991 and, by the end of February 2019, has published 106 books of poetry, fiction, non-fiction, literary translation, and literary criticism in English and Chinese. Ouyang's poetry has been included in the *Best Australian Poetry* collections for 11 times from 2004 to 2016. He has published five English novels to date, *The Eastern Slope Chronicle* (2002), *The English Class* (2010), *Loose: A Wild History* (2011), *Diary of a Naked Official* (2014), and *Billy Sing* (2017), and five Chinese novels, *The Angry Wu Zili* (1999 and 2016), *Land of Gold-diggers* (2014), *A Lonely Night Boat* (2016 in Taiwan), *She* (2017), and *The Colour Green [Vols. I, II and III]* (a trilogy, 2018). He was nominated one of the Top 100 Most Influential Melbournians in

2011 as well as the Top 10 Most Influential Writers of Chinese Origin of the Chinese Diaspora. Since 2012, he has been the "Siyuan Scholar" and a professor of English at Shanghai University of International Business and Economics.

Jami Proctor Xu is a bilingual poet, mother and translator. She writes in English and Chinese and splits her time between Northern California, Arizona and China. Her publications include, among others, a Chinese chapbook *Shimmers* (EMS, 2013) a Chinese poetry collection *Suddenly Starting to Dance* (Yi, 2016), an English chapbook *Hummingbird Ignites a Star*, the translated collection of Jidi Majia *Words from the Fire* (Manoa, 2018), and the translated collection of Song Lin *Sunday Sparrows* (Zephyr, 2019). Since 2016, she has co-organized an annual international poetry exchange at Beijing Normal University's International Writing Center, and since 2019, she has collaborated with Zolani Mkiva to co-organize international poetry events in South Africa. She frequently reads at festivals around the world, and her work has been published in anthologies in several languages. She is a recipient of the Zhujiang Poetry Award (2013), the First Reader Best Poet Award (2016), and a recipient of a Northern California Book Award for Poetry in Translation for Sunday Sparrows (2020).

Margaret Ross's first book of poetry, *A Timeshare*, was published in 2015. Her poems and translations have appeared in *A Public Space, Boston Review, The New Republic*, and *The New Yorker.* Her honors include scholarships and fellowships from the Fulbright Program, the Bread Loaf Writers' Conference, the Iowa Writers' Workshop, and Stanford, where she is currently a Stegner Fellow.

Susan M. Schultz is an American poet, critic, publisher and English professor at the University of Hawaii in Manoa. She specializes in modern and contemporary poetry, American literature, and creative writing.

James Sherry is the author of 13 books of poetry and prose, most recently *The Oligarch* (Palgrave MacMillan, 2017) and the poetry book *Entangled Bank* (Chax Press, 2016). His essay book *Selfie: Poetry & Ecology* is forthcoming from Palgrave in 2021. Since 1976, he has edited Roof Books and Roof Magazine, publishing more than 200 titles of seminal works of language writing, flarf, conceptual poetry, new narrative, and environmental poetry. He started The Segue Foundation, Inc. in 1977, producing over 10,000 events of poetry and other arts in New York City.

Diana Shi's renderings of Chinese language, contemporary American, and other poetry have appeared widely East and West. With George O'Connell, she edited and translated the 2008 *Atlanta Review* China Issue. Their 2017 release, *Darkening Mirror: New & Selected Poems* by Wang Jiaxin, is currently shortlisted for the American Literary Translators Association Lucien Stryk Prize. *Crossing the Harbour*, their bilingual anthology of ten contemporary

Hong Kong Chinese-language poets, appeared the same year. Co-recipient of a U.S. National Endowment for the Arts Literature Fellowship in Translation, and two Hong Kong Arts Development Council awards, Ms. Shi also received the Chinese University of Hong Kong's Dawson Lee Memorial Prize.

Jordan A.Y. Smith is a translator, writer, and associate professor of comparative literature and translation studies. He has translated many of Japan's veteran and cutting-edge poets, including Yoshimasu Gozo, Tanikawa Shuntaro, Mizuta Noriko, Miki Yuuri, Saihate Tahi, Kanie Naha, and Nagae Yuki. He also writes poetry (solo volume: *Syzygy*, Awai Books) and has co-authored two volumes *√IC:Redux* (2018) and *Sea of Trees: Poetic Gateways to Aokigahara* (2019). Co-editor of *Tokyo Poetry Journal*. Poetry Slam Japan, National Finalist (2017, 2018). Organizer of KOTOBA Slam Japan and co-founder of the Cōem collective for coding+poetry.
Josh Stenberg is a lecturer in Chinese Studies at the University of Sydney, writer, and translator. Besides literary translation, his research interests include Chinese theatre, Southeast Asian Chinese communities, and transnational literature and performance. He has translated or edited four volumes of contemporary Chinese literature. His monograph *Minority Stages: Sino-Indonesian Performance and Public Display* is forthcoming with University of Hawai'i Press.

Daniel Tay is an actor, translator, and aspiring medical doctor from New York City. He was born in 1991, and received his BA from Yale University in 2014. He has won the Richard U. Light Fellowship and the Maurice R. Greenberg Scholarship for his studies in Mandarin Chinese. Co-authored with Xin Xu, his translation of Zhang Dai's "Night Opera in Jinshan" won the Aetna Translation Award from University of Connecticut in 2019.

Jeremy Tiang's translations from Chinese include novels by Su Wei-Chen, Zhang Yueran, Chan Ho-Kei, Yeng Pway Ngon, and Li Er, as well as nonfiction by Yu Qiuyu and Jackie Chan. He also writes and translates plays, and is the author of a short story collection, *It Never Rains on National Day*, and a novel, *State of Emergency*, which won the Singapore Literature Prize. He is the managing editor of *Pathlight* and a founding member of Cedilla & Co., a collective of literary translators.

Jeffrey Twitchell-Waas currently lives in Malta and edits the *Z-site* (www.z-site.net) on the work of Louis Zukofsky.

Austin Woerner is a translator of contemporary Chinese poetry and fiction and has published translations in *Poetry*, *Kenyon Review Online*, *Zoland Poetry*, and elsewhere. The recipient of fellowships from the Vermont Studio Center and the UC Riverside Department of Comparative Literature, he holds a degree in East Asian Studies from Yale University and lives in New York City.

Penny Fang Xia is a translator and received a PhD in Creative Writing from the Department of English, University of Macao.

Joan Xie was born in Shanghai where she attended Shanghai Jiaotong University. She came to the United States in 1988 to study business and law. She established her law practice in New York City in 2000, specializing in immigration law. She is a prolific writer of poetry and essays, both in English and Chinese, as well as a poetry translator of both languages. Xie's poetry and essay collections include *Half-Century Journey* (catalogue with poetry, 2015), *Looking Back* (essay, 2016), *Nothing Made Me Happier than Finding These Objects* (Beiyue Literature and Art Publishing House, 2018), *Thirteen Leaves—Selected Poems of Contemporary Chinese Poets* (Three Owls Press, 2018). An award winner at First Moganshan International Poetry Festival in China, her works have been widely published in leading poetry journals at both China and the United States. She is currently also deputy editor of International Poetry Exchange, chairman of X Poetry Club, and legal consultant of American Overseas Chinese PEN and *New York Poetry Journal.*

Xuan Yuan earned her Master's Degree in linguistics at Guangxi University in Nanning and has been teaching at the same university since then. She was a visiting scholar at Morehead State University in United States in 2012. Besides language teaching, she also works on literary translation.

Yang Yujun is an English teacher, poet, and translator. She was born in Beijing and currently lives in Taishan, Guangdong. Her poems first appeared in newspapers and magazines in 1986, and she has since written and translated various works totaling 7 million words including two collections of short stories by Alice Munro. Her collections of Chinese and English poems include *Garden in Winter* and *The Hand On The Mouse Is Turning Cold.* She has translated about 20 collections of poems by other Chinese poets namely Shen Qi, Huang Lihai, Ma Yongbo, Zhou Lunyou, Chen Zhiyun, Yu Tian, and Yanrong.

Zhang Dongying is a lecturer and PhD candidate at School of Foreign Languages, Central China Normal University. She was a 2015-2016 Fulbright Foreign Language Teaching Assistant (FLTA) at the University of Notre Dame. She is academically interested in British and American Literature, Poetry and Poetics, and Literary Translation.

Zhang Qin was born in 1980. She is an associate professor at the School of Foreign Languages and a PhD candidate of English languages and literature at Central China Normal University in Wuhan, Hubei Province. She was a visiting scholar at Chapman University in the United States, financed by the Fulbright FLTA program 2009-2010. Her academic interest is contemporary Chinese American literature.

Acknowledgments:

Zhou Zan
"Mr. Zhang San Rides through Town on a Minibus." *Another Kind of Nation: An Anthology of Contemporary Chinese Poetry*, edited by Zhang Er and Chen Dongdong, Talisman House, Publishers, 2007.

Zang Di
"Spinach," *Greenmarket Poetry Series* (Sept. 2015).
"After the New Society for Wisdom." *Best American Poetry blog*, (Sept. 16, 2013).
The Roots of Wisdom Series: Selected Poems of Zang Di, Zephyr Press (Oct. 2017). All poems with the exception of "Spinach."

Chen Dongdong
Ten poems in *Ancient Enmity: An Anthology of the Hong Kong International Poetry Nights 2015* (Hong Kong: The Chinese University Press, 2017).

Un Sio San and Jeremy Tiang
"Nude Picnic." *Two Lines*, Issue 24, March 2016 and "Dogtrack." *Manoa*, vol. 31 no. 1, 2019, p. 121-121. *Project MUSE*, doi:10.1353/man.2019.0068.
"Mrs. Robinson at the Hotel Estoril," translated by Jeremy Tiang. *Words Without Borders*, August 2018. Translation © 2018 by Jeremy Tiang. By permission of *Words Without Borders*. All rights reserved.